Harry Edward Shenton Jr., Fort Hancock, Georgia
Spring 1918

The Lost SketchBOOKS

A Young Artist in The Great War

by Rex Passion
with drawings
by Edward Shenton

Published in the United States of America in 2014
by Komatik Press, Torbay Bight Companies, Inc.
95 Jackson Street, Cambridge, Massachusetts 02140
www.komatikpress.com

and in Canada by
Komatik Press, Torbay Bight Companies, Inc.
62 Lower Street, Torbay, Newfoundland and Labrador A1K 1B3

ISBN: 978-0-9828219-5-4

Printed and bound in Canada
design by Vis-à-Vis Graphics

Publisher's Cataloging-in-Publication data
Passion, Rex.
    The Lost sketchbooks : a young artist in the great war / by Rex Passion ;
Illustrated by Edward Shenton.
    p. cm.
    ISBN 978-9828219-5-4
1.Shenton, Edward, 1895-1977. 2. World War, 1914-1918—Art and
the war.
3. War Artists. 4. War in art. I. Shenton, Edward, 1895-1977. II. Title.

N8260.P37 2014
709.04/1 –dc23   20144909009

THE LOST SKETCHBOOKS

Komatik
Press

Cambridge
St. John's

This poem was written at the bottom of the watercolor used for the cover:

I have watched for a thousand days and nights
The star-shells over No-Mans-Land
Where death stalks with his shadowy shears
To clip the final quivering strand.

Contents

Maps

INTRODUCTION

On the moonless night of July 8, 1918 twenty-two-year-old corporal Edward Shenton of Company B, 103rd Engineers, 28th Division, of the American Expeditionary Force crouched in a shallow trench above the Marne River near Citry, France. He watched the artillery duel around the nearby town of Château Thierry expecting some sort of attack, but the romantic beauty of the distant battle eclipsed any sense of fear.

Corporal Shenton gazed at the smoke from the burning town, highlighted by flares floating in the dark sky. In his mind he pictured medieval knights with leveled lances charging toward massed ranks of Godless enemies, the dust from their horses' hooves glowing on the horizon.

Years earlier, when he first read Arthur Conan Doyle's stories of knights errant, he imagined himself as Sir Nigel Loring in the vanguard of the White Company, charging toward rival hordes, determined to vanquish his enemies and win honor for his Lady. Now he was in France, and the war he had signed up for was about to get very real.

Ninety-one years later his son, Ned, came to me and said he wanted to do a small biography about his father, who became one of the foremost book and magazine illustrators of his time. Unlike his contemporaries, Rockwell Kent and Maxfield Parish, he was little known outside the illustration community and Ned wanted to celebrate his life. I agreed and he brought over boxes full of his father's papers and artwork. Among them were nine small canvas-covered books that looked very interesting.

They turned out to be the sketchbooks that his father had carried with him from the time he joined the Pennsylvania National Guard in 1917, throughout his time as a combat engineer in France, until he returned home in 1919. The drawings were fantastic, and I had the idea that one day I would do a book using Ed's sketches.

The small biography was printed in 2010 and Ned and I went on to do one about his mother, Barbara Webster, but my idea of a book from the sketches kept growing. When I decided to go ahead with the project, I asked Ned to bring back the sketchbooks I had scanned earlier. I was not sure if the order of my scans corresponded with the order of the drawings and I wanted to double check. When he delivered a box full of sketchbooks, none of the ones I had seen before was among them and there were eleven additional ones. I now had a total of twenty sketchbooks and nearly 300 loose drawings from Ed's time in the army, none of which had been seen for over ninety years!

The next thing I needed was some way to put the sketches into context. I came across a book, long out of print, written by three officers from Ed's unit in the army. Published in 1929, *Soldiers of the Castle, A History of Company B, Engineer Battalion, National Guard of Pennsylvania* by J. H. M. Andrews, J. S. Bradford and Charles Elcock, gives a day-by-day description of where the company was located, what the men were doing, and, to a small extent, what they were feeling, from their first day in training camp until they were discharged in May, 1919.

Soldiers was a fantastic find and I knew I had an opportunity to give a personal account of one man's experiences in The Great War. In January, 2014, Ned gave me permission to publish his father's sketches and I was off and running.

I decided to use the sequence of places and events detailed in *Soldiers of the Castle* for the narrative of Ed's story. Many of the dates and locations he included in his sketches correspond exactly with those in *Soldiers* so I was comfortable with this decision. Rarely did a drawing have a date and place different than that given in the book, but individual platoons and squads

were sometimes detached from the rest of the company, so that made sense.

In a few instances there are no drawings of certain places and events. Although the battles of Saint-Agnan and Fismes are well documented, his time at Charly-sur-Marne and in the Argonne are less so. There are no sketches from the boat trip to France, and this is puzzling. He had a good deal of time on his hands, a full complement of drawing materials and lots of interesting subjects. Perhaps there is a sketchbook that is yet to be found.

During the process of trying to imagine what Ed and the men of Company B were seeing on their journey through France, I made frequent use of the Street View feature of Google Earth. With it I could see the countryside through which they rode or marched and, as rural France has changed little over the last 100 years, see the sights as they would have seen them.

In my effort to present as closely as possible the look of Ed's original sketches, I have done little to adjust the images. I left most of the blemishes that were on the pages when I first saw them in 2009. In the end, I was able to include 150 of the more than 500 sketches he drew in his two years of service with Company B.

None of Ed's wartime correspondence to his family has been found and so his sketches tell his story. There are two "letters" published in his high school magazine, *The Western*, and several stories and poems related to his wartime experiences which he wrote after his return home, but little else. He did not keep a diary during the war, so his sketches are one of the few documents that give insight into his time in the army.

Ed regularly sent his sketchbooks back to his father in Philadelphia and several of his drawings were published in six separate issues of *The Philadelphia Record* from February of 1918 to June of 1919, and in at least one issue of *The Philadelphia Evening Public Ledger.*

When he returned home he tried to tell his stories, and show his sketchbooks but no one was interested in the war. In Philadelphia he continued his art studies and his career began to take off. He packed away his wartime sketchbooks and forgot about them; they did not see the light of day for over nine decades.

Throughout history armies have employed artists. Winslow Homer and Thomas Nast drew Civil War scenes while John Singer Sargent was among a dozen or so who did the same in World War I, but they were not soldiers. They did not have the perspective of someone who did their artwork in the midst of battle.

During the war Ed Shenton was a foot soldier who carried everything on his back and followed the orders of his superiors. He was trained to kill with the rifle, bayonet and hand grenade; to march through the mud and hastily dig a hole in which to hide. When he was at the front, the only drawing tools he had available were a pencil and a sketchbook, and even that he cut in half. The time he had to draw was limited to when he was not digging trenches or building bridges or repairing roads. He had to draw on the fly and was proud of the fact that he could create a composition in thirty seconds. Ed's drawings have an immediacy that is seldom seen in professional war artists.

The Lost Sketchbooks, A Young Artist in The Great War is the personal account of a man who, from a young age, had a talent for drawing what he saw, or what he imagined. Like so many men of his generation he was caught up with the excitement of the worldwide conflict. Taking his romantic ideas of war and a load of sketchbooks with him, sailed off to Europe for a grand adventure. Whether he intended it or not, his drawings tell the story of that adventure.

THE EARLY YEARS

001 *Battling Ships and Drowning Sailors*

Harry Edward Shenton Jr. was born in Pottstown, Pennsylvania on November 29, 1895. His father was a stonecutter and designer of monuments and H. E. Jr. grew up among the sketches of his father's work.

His earliest known drawings, done in 1905 at the age of nine, are scenes of warriors locked in intense combat, horribly wounding one another with swords, rifles and pistols, the flags of the United States and Spain flying prominently above the battlefield. There are sketches of soldiers attacking a fort with cannons and burning their enemies' tents; of sea battles, schooners with huge sails and raked masts, armored ships bristling with guns and sailors struggling in the floating debris.

That same year Japan annihilated the Russian fleet at the Battle of Tsushima, and Britain was building the first modern battleship. Theodore Roosevelt was president and Harry was in the fourth grade at Sadie Hanna Grammar School in Philadelphia. The Spanish American War was still a fresh memory and perhaps his class was studying that recent American triumph while he was doodling figures of Teddy leading the charge up San Juan Hill.

At age 12, Harry came down with rheumatic fever and was confined to his bed. During the next two years he spent hours reading books about medieval history and the adventures of such heroes as Ian Maclaren's "Graham of Claverhouse," Arthur Conan Doyle's "Sir Nigel Loring" and G. A. Henty's "Sir Walter Somers." He became enthralled with the deeds of these warriors, the details of their equipment and the battles they fought. He made hundreds of drawings of scenes from the books he read.

After recovering his health, Harry, now fifteen, decided to change his name. He got rid of the "Harry," which he had disliked for years, and instead used the shortened version of his middle name and called himself Ed.

002 *Teddy Roosevelt*
003 *Sir Nigel Loring*

About this time he became interested in the emerging sport of auto racing. He read *The Philadelphia Evening Telegraph*, eagerly awaiting the results of the weekend's countrywide races. He and his younger brother, Don, went to the events at the Point Breeze track across the Schuylkill River from their West Philadelphia home. In 1911 he produced a series of monthly, hand-drawn and lettered booklets, typically twelve pages long, that were a vivid expression of his passion for car racing.

↖**004** *Graham of Claverhouse*
↓**005** *Around the Repair Camps*

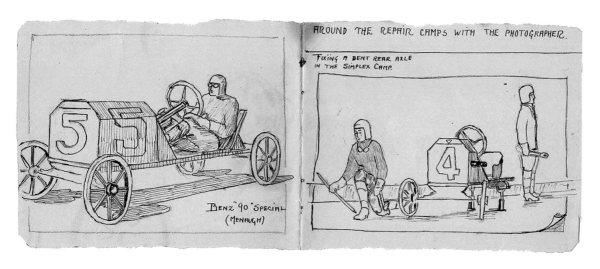

DAVID BRUCE-BROWN (Am)

In addition to auto racing news, these booklets told the fictitious tale of the careers of D. T. and H. E. Shenton (D. T. was Ed's brother, Don) who were chief drivers and shameless promoters of Simplex motorcars. *Simplex Cars on Road and Track* is full of the exploits of these two drivers as they competed in the 55th St. Hill Climb, a wholly made up monthly event that started at their driveway and which they usually won. The drawings in some of these booklets show a remarkably well developed talent for perspective drawing and shading.

↓ **006** Simplex Cars on Road and Track, *April 1911 Cover*
← **007** Motor Car Record *Vol. II*

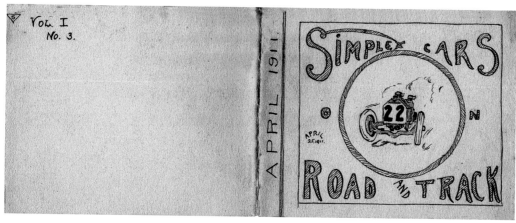

VOL. I
NO. 3.

APRIL 1911

SIMPLEX CARS
ON
ROAD AND TRACK

APRIL
25.1911.

008 Le Magasin des Follies

009 *The Queen's Revenge*

In September, 1912 the West Philadelphia High School for Boys opened at 48ᵗʰ and Walnut Streets. It was built to relieve the overcrowding of other schools, among them Central Manual Training High School, which both Ed and Don attended.

While in high school, possibly for an art class project, Ed wrote and illustrated *Le Magasin des Folies*. "Published Every Fortnight" in 1912 and 1913, the magazine was created by a wonderfully fictitious staff such as Editor Edwardo Clap-Saddle and Assistant Bettina Bun Bun; the illustrator was none other than the "rising young artist," Payne Page. There are ads for Locomobile, "The Best Built Car in America," a story by Madem Punk Noodle and a poem by Dreamer D. Dippy.

A Four day beard!
and a boil!
Barnegat City.

In his first year at West Philly High, Ed joined the staff of the school's magazine, and over four years he contributed many drawings and stories to *The Western*. He was feeling pretty good about himself in the summer of 1914 when he and Don were sailing along the Jersey Shore, but across the sea the world was starting to unravel. Ed may have been aware of the assassination of the heir to the Austro-Hungarian throne on June 28, but there is no hint of it in his writings or sketches.

Yacht
Mable
Island Heights.
June 3rd 1914

←**010** *A Four Day Beard and a Boil*
↑**011** *"Yacht"* Mable

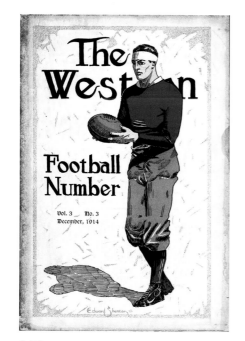

012 The Western, *December 1914*

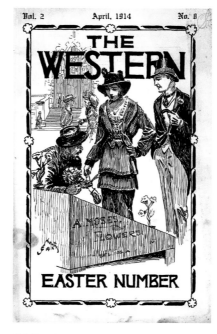

013 The Western, *April 1914*

014 The Western, *October 1914 Frontispiece*

When he returned to school in the fall as a junior, Ed was chosen as Editor-in-Chief of *The Western*. In addition to drawings for section headings and cartoons, he was now responsible for the total content of the magazine. He illustrated stories for each issue, some written by him and some by others.

His tales were mostly about daring men in airplanes, race cars or speedboats, winning the esteem of beautiful young women; or of romantic heartbreaks, both of which appealed to his high school readers. Occasionally he even applied his flowery prose to sports but there is one story in the October, 1914 issue which combines chivalric romance with vivid descriptions of the horrors of the battlefield.

In the summer of 1915, Ed enrolled at the Pennsylvania Museum and School of Industrial Arts and his classes continued during the winter break of 1915 – 1916. There is a canvas-bound sketchbook with two sections; the first, "The Rogues Gallery", consisting of pen and ink drawings interspersed with poetry. The "mascot" of this section is a character named Prison Posey. He appears in all but two of the twelve drawings done between July 1 and September 5, 1915. Often forlorn, he wears striped garb and is seen behind bars, breaking rocks, chained to a ball or hanging from a scaffold; in one picture he is on his knees admiring a glowing cross. A page carefully lettered, "Sketch Class of the School of Industrial Art" introduces the second half, which contains classroom drawings of various models.

015 *Rogues Gallery*

016 *Edith Ogden*

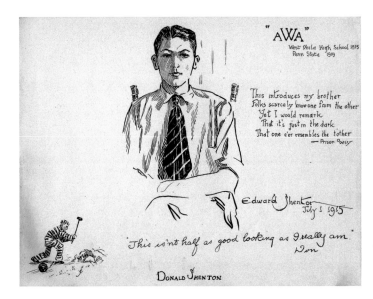

017 *Don Shenton*

Although Dan was two-years younger and more handsome, Ed was more talented and popular. They both worked on *The Western*, Ed as Editor-in-Chief and Don as a columnist. They were partners in the racing magazine and both shared in "driving" the Simplex "Red Devil," but Don was always in Ed's shadow. In a page from *Simplex Cars on Road and Track* dated May, 1911, a somewhat sad-looking H. T.

Shenton, "crack driver of the Simplex," laid down his racing gloves in favor of his younger brother, the confident D. T. Evidently H. E. came out of retirement as both he and D. T. were noted as driving the car in later issues. During Ed's senior year, Don graduated and went away to Penn State.

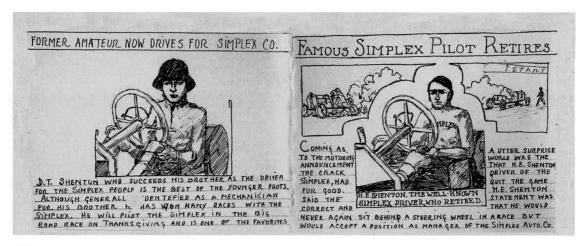

018 *Famous Simplex Pilot Retires*

When Ed graduated in February of 1916 he had been class vice president for one year and president for two. He was Art Editor of *The Western* in 1912 and 1913 and its Editor-in-Chief for 1914 and 1915; he was Class Poet and cheerleader. Most extraordinary of all, despite, or rather because of, his slight size, he was able to earn a "W" as the coxswain of the 1915 rowing team.

Thanks to his art studies, both at West Philly High and the Museum School, he was well on his way to becoming an accomplished artist and illustrator. He was satisfied with who he was and where he was going in life.

ENLISTMENT

After graduation Ed enrolled at the Museum School full time, but his experience was far different from high school. He was no longer the top of the heap; he was not class president nor magazine editor nor class poet. He was only one art student among many.

This time in his life was difficult. There is a notebook from the fall and winter of 1916 with a worn black cover and broken binding that contains numerous drawings, many incomplete, some only outlines. Among the sketches there are pages of writing, some stories, some poems; many laments of lost loves and confessions of inadequacy.

On one page is a poem that seems to best express his melancholy. In the margin is written: "Lonely   Lonly" as if he were trying out the spelling of the word.

Here are the melancholy castles I have built,
The battlements are down, a tower falls,
The rooks fly in and down the crumbling walls,
Dust gathers in the crannys and the silt,
Weaves patterns when the wind blows down the halls.

There's not a roof to shelter You from rain,
And silver pools shine on the flag-stone floors,
The rusty hinges creak on swinging doors.

Poor dismal castles that I built in Spain,
Far higher than the lonely eagle soars.

How can you want them with each empty room,
And vacant windows staring at the sky?
The weeds grow in the silent court waist high,
The dripping corridors are wrapped in gloom,
These are my castles: pass them by.

019 *The Skull*

Throughout the year Ed continued his art studies and wrote his gloomy stories while in February the longest and bloodiest battle of the war began at Verdun. It would last for ten months and extinguish the lives of nearly 300,000 soldiers, but for young men isolated in the United States, life went on without interruption, until the next winter.

Although President Wilson had been against intervention in the European conflict, and indeed had tried several times to broker a peace between the belligerents, in the winter of 1916 – 1917 circumstances aligned which forced him to break diplomatic relations and eventually, on April 6, 1917, to ask Congress for a Declaration of War with Germany.

That same spring, in a small booklet of poems, Ed envisioned himself as a creature called a Mug-Wamp, someone who is caught on a fence, "with his Mug on one side and his Wamp on the other," but despite a period of doubt, he had made a decision and, "Answering when the bugle blows to join the greatest game," he enlisted in the National Guard.

Whether it was the springtime, or a new romance or the fact that he had made a decision, Ed was back to his old high school self. This poem, entitled "The Egotist" is from the Mug-Wamp booklet:

I gaze about the lunch-room at noon-time when I dine
And heave a sigh for all the girls that never can be mine
I soak my bread in weakened tea and sip a silent toast
While their faces pass before me in a never ending host.

Poor dears I know the agony that fills their dreams at night
And all they'd like to say to me when I am out of sight.
Eyes of blue and black and brown that never more will shine
Poor dears, oh, lonesome dears that never can be mine.

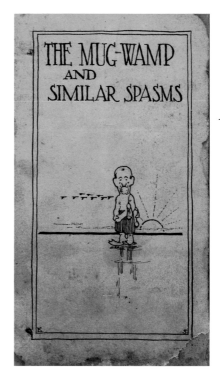

A MUG-WAMP MOME : Recording Emotions of Departure. A True Study.

HANG all the flags at quarter-mast
The Mug-Wamp's going away to war
Oh drop a tear within the soup
And fan the cabbages once more.

Stand up and drink a silent toast
Of India-Ink and shaving-soap
And wipe your chin upon your plate
And watch the macaroons elope

Come! Turn the butter upside down
And heave the chicken out the door
Then clamber in the gravy bowl
The Mug-Wamp's going away to war.

↑ **020** *Mug-Wamp*
↗ **021** *Mug-Wamp Goes to War*

Ed Shenton was a romantic and despite what he read of the horrors in the trenches and on the battlefields of France, when he and fifteen of his high school friends, including his brother, Don, enlisted in the Pennsylvania National Guard he saw himself joining a virtuous crusade. In his heart of hearts he imagined he was going to France with The White Company on a great knightly errand, with his closest comrades at his side.

On April 18, 1917 Ed joined the 103rd Engineer Regiment at their armory in Philadelphia and was assigned to Company B; when he sailed to France, the 103rd was attached to the 28th Division of the American Expeditionary Force. Ironically, his grandfather had joined Company A of the 6th Regiment of the Pennsylvania Guard almost exactly forty years earlier.

The 103rd Engineers can trace their history back to the Associators of Philadelphia, a combined artillery company put together by Benjamin Franklin in 1747 to guard the harbor. In 1909 they existed as Company A of the Engineering Battalion of the National Guard in Scranton, Pennsylvania. Seeing the high esteem in which the citizens of Philadelphia held Company A when they marched through their streets, members of the Governor's staff and the Engineers Club decided they needed to form a similar unit and thus, on January 8, 1909 Company B was born.

The Company was mustered into Federal service on June 29, 1916, and was sent to the Southwest. In what turned out to be a practice for the war in Europe, they were off to chase Pancho Villa on the border of Mexico. They never did find Villa, nor did they ever chase him for that matter, but they learned how to pack up and move in a hurry, to march in the dark; how to repair roads, build bridges and map the countryside. Although they never fired a shot in anger, they drilled as infantry and practiced with their rifles. In a war game exercise, the advance guard of Company B was hypothetically wiped out by machine gun fire. Their border expedition was good training, good practice; frequently good fun and, from time to time even accompanied by good food.

The 103rd Engineers' first response to the declaration of war in 1917 was to increase its recruitment and within two weeks, Ed and Don and their friends from West Philly High had taken the oath, pledging their lives to both the Commonwealth of Pennsylvania and to the United States of America.

For the next two months, they trained periodically as National Guard soldiers drilling on a dusty vacant lot near the armory. The recruits kept their civilian jobs; Ed remained enrolled at the Museum School and Don stayed at Penn State. Some of the men who joined in Philadelphia were selected to make up the new Company E, Don among them, the rest remained in Company B. On June 26 the regiment was once again called up and summoned into Federal service, this time for a real war and the company made preparations to move into training camp.

Before Ed left home, he stopped by John Wanamaker's Department Store and stocked up on artist's supplies. He did not know how long it would be before he could get more and he knew he was going to do a lot of drawing in this great adventure. He spent all morning buying pencils, graphite sticks, loose paper and a watercolor set. Most importantly he bought a large number of canvas covered sketchbooks emblazoned in red script on the front with the word "Sketches." He carried them with him for the next two years. They were packed in his kit, cut in half, carried in the pocket of his trench coat, and mailed back to his father in Philadelphia.

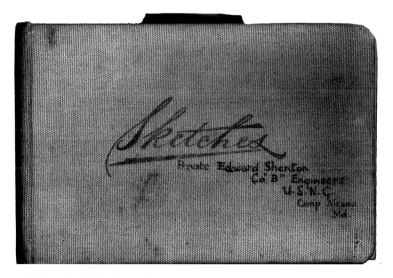

022 *Meade Sketchbook Cover*

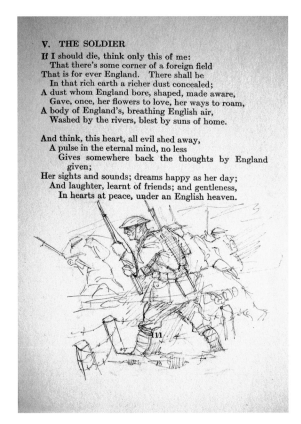

V. THE SOLDIER

If I should die, think only this of me:
  That there's some corner of a foreign field
That is for ever England.   There shall be
  In that rich earth a richer dust concealed;
A dust whom England bore, shaped, made aware,
  Gave, once, her flowers to love, her ways to roam,
A body of England's, breathing English air,
  Washed by the rivers, blest by suns of home.

And think, this heart, all evil shed away,
  A pulse in the eternal mind, no less
    Gives somewhere back the thoughts by England
      given;
  Her sights and sounds; dreams happy as her day;
    And laughter, learnt of friends; and gentleness,
      In hearts at peace, under an English heaven.

023   *Ruppert Brooke*

Among his other treasures was a copy of *The Collected Poems of Rupert Brooke*, given to him at Christmas by a friend. Below the fifth of Brooke's 1914 sonnets, entitled "The Soldier," Ed sketched a bayonet-wielding infantrymen charging through barbed wire. Along with his canvas-bound sketchbooks, Ed carried this book of poems with him throughout France.

024 *July 4th Pup Tent*

LEARNING TO BE A SOLDIER
Camp Meade

On July 4, 1917 Company B arrived in Maryland by train and set up their pup tents next to a large vegetable garden. They were among the first units of the Pennsylvania National Guard to take the field in the war. The site of their training camp was still raw land, and the equally raw soldiers literally "took the field" and started their training by camping out, and then, of course, it started to rain. Many soldiers spent considerable time sleeping on the ground in pup tents. Even when well pitched and with a ditch to divert rainwater, their occupants were often damp in all but the most severe rainstorms, when they were flooded out.

Company B was extremely fortunate – or very well prepared – and the men spent only three soggy nights in their pup tents. Their pyramid tents, each equipped with a wooden floor,

Repairing Ventolators

← **025** *Repairing Ventilators*
↑ **026** *Johnny Armstrong with Newspaper*

arrived promptly. They had vertical walls making them relatively roomy and sides, which could be rolled up in hot weather. They were vented at the top and accommodated a wood stove; eight men could sleep comfortably on wooden cots and remain dry.

In the spring of 1917 America was wholly unprepared for world conflict. When war was declared, rifles were scarce and few machine guns were available for combat training. American artillery was still in the design stages and would not be available for combat until late in 1918. There were not enough uniforms and only a few training camps.

027 *Well No 2.*

028 *The Road Builders*

The spring and summer of 1917 was a time of catching up, with building going on at a fever pitch. Only one week before the men boarded the train in Philadelphia, the federal government had chosen the site for what was to become Camp Meade and had purchased land at Admiral, Maryland, between Baltimore and Washington. When Company B arrived, it was difficult to envision how the army could be ready to fight any time soon.

Camp Meade itself was being constructed by contractors who established the roads and dug the wells. There was a constant buzz of building activity and many pieces of machinery at work at all hours of the day.

An Engineer doing his daily "drill"

An 'Engineer'

029 *An Engeneer's Daily Drill*

While all this was going on, the soldiers were learning how to excavate trenches and erect barbed wire barriers. Most of their time was taken up with practicing these engineering skills, along with the seemingly endless drilling, marching and inspections. The men who joined with Ed had learned much of their basic military protocol in Philadelphia. How and who to salute, and how to march in groups with order and precision were all taught at the armory. When they got to Maryland they learned how to dig.

They practiced with picks and shovels and were taught how to work in teams to construct large trench works. They felled trees and cut the logs with two-man saws. They learned how to use their entrenching tool to quickly dig a hole in which to hide when bullets came their way. They became proficient with hatchets, crowbars, mauls and wire cutters.

The use of massed artillery and the machine gun had forced soldiers to shelter underground as they never had before and in 1914 the study of a new kind of warfare was hastily begun. For the previous three years, the British had been learning trench construction on the job. In 1917 *Field Entrenchments*, a revision of the British manual, became available to American engineers, and soldiers began digging in training camps across the country.

The officers as well as the men were studying this new craft. They found out how long men could work and how close to one another they could dig; how the quality of the soil, the climate and the men's condition affected the quantity of earth they moved. They studied charts, maps and diagrams and learned where to dig and what type of fortifications to construct. They eventually acquired the ability to interpret the orders of their superiors into detailed directions for their men.

The week at Camp Meade was Monday to Friday with trench work, marching, calisthenics and hiking, but the weekends were free time. The men could wash their clothes – a task that some young soldiers had to learn – and take care of personal business. There was a good deal of entertainment provided by nearby residents including dances, group singing, and musical and theatrical performances. Soldiers were also allowed to take the trolley to towns as far away as Baltimore. The residents of Odenton, the nearby town, were very hospitable toward the thousands of visiting troops, inviting them into their homes for Sunday dinners. At nights the soldiers often engaged in pastimes dear to their hearts.

↗ **030** *The Pick and Shovel Gang*
→ **031** *The Gamblers*

Few things are more important to a soldier's sense of well being than his food, and throughout his time in the army, Ed paid a good deal of attention to how the soldiers got their meals. The company had the best cooks in the regiment, and their own kitchen wagon that stayed with them until after the end of the war. Whenever it was possible, the men ate well.

Their location next to a truck garden was a great boon. Not only did the cooks have easy access to fresh vegetables, they were able to trade them for credit at the engineers' canteen where the men could then get treats such as candy or cigarettes. The vegetable credits lasted well into their stay at their next camp.

At the end of August, the engineers were ordered to move from Camp Meade to Camp Hancock near Augusta, Georgia. They had been in Maryland for two months and had learned a great deal about being a soldier and a combat engineer. They had worked hard during the week, and had a good time on the weekends, but things were about to change.

034 *The Baggage Pile*

Company Street

Camp Hancock

Today the land that was once Camp Hancock is a quiet residential suburb of Augusta, Georgia, planted with oaks and hickories, but in the summer of 1917 it was a flat sandy plain with no trees but longleaf pines.

By September 3 the men of Company B occupied a city of pyramid tents where they slept comfortably on wood and canvas cots. There were buildings for mess halls, showers, latrines and infirmaries; there was running water and electricity and fresh bread daily from a massive field bakery. All in all it was a pretty nice place to live, at least for the time being.

Despite Ed's early doubts after joining the National Guard, he was now enthusiastic about learning to be a soldier. He knew he could do his training and still have time to draw. He was surrounded by friends whom he had known for years and who shared his anticipation of their upcoming enterprise. He had been elevated to the rank of corporal and as such, was the leader of a squad of men. He felt like a young squire learning his knightly trade among his fellows.

← **035** *Company Street*

Field Bakery.   30,000 loaves per day.

036   *Field Bakery*

Edward Shenton
Co B 103 Engs.
Camp Hancock
Augusta
APRIL, 1918.   Ga

As Ed and his friends were getting settled into Camp Hancock, and the rains were turning the Georgia roads to red mud, the British and Canadians were launching an attack in Flanders. In the Belgian town of Passchendaele it was raining as well, and days of artillery bombardment had turned it and the surrounding countryside into a boggy moonscape where thousands died in the deep mud. In Georgia the training went on and the time grew nearer when Ed and his friends would have their chance at war.

In the fall of 1917 the engineers of Company B began their training in earnest. They were now working six days a week, from morning reveille intil evening retreat, with only Sundays and holidays for themselves. They had calisthenics early in the morning, half-hour physical training sessions throughout the day and frequent hikes of four or five miles with full packs.

As mapmaking was a crucial task, the company was introduced to the art of cartography. They went on long survey hikes practicing with the compass, sextant and various mathematical tables to make accurate battlefield maps. The experienced engineer officers had done a plane table survey of Camp Meade and continued their work at Hancock.

→ **037** *Survey Party*

Survey Party

→ **038** *Bomb Proof Trench Work*

↘ **039** *Napping in the Trenches*

Using the *Engineers Field Manual* the men were taught how to build bridges, roads, and fortifications. They practiced stringing barbed wire, erecting camouflage netting and constructing various obstacles that would impede the enemy. For each thing they built, they also studied how to overcome or destroy it.

In Maryland they had learned the basic art of trench building; in Georgia they exercised their talents again and again and were becoming accomplished excavators. Dugouts roofed with logs and sandbags to protect against direct shellfire, loopholes where riflemen could shoot the enemy without being shot in return and trenches covered with sheet metal to protect the men from bullets and burst shells had all became part of their repertoire. They dug miles of fire trenches, reserve trenches and communication trenches, so when it was time to dig in earnest, their actions were automatic. By the time they left for France, they were also experts in concealment, deception and camouflage.

Napping in the Trenches.

Shooting silhouettes on the 200 yd.

040 *Shooting Silhouettes*

041 *Two Riflemen*

The men of Company B were first of all soldiers, and their training as infantrymen was at least as intense as their schooling as engineers; rifle handling was at the center of that training. They spent hours drilling with their Model 1903 Springfields learning how to manipulate them according to the standard manual of arms. They were shown how to fix and unfix their bayonets and adjust their slings and then performed these tasks over and over. They studied the detailed steps of adjusting their sights to account for wind and the idiosyncrasies of both the gun and the shooter. Inevitably they were awkward at first, but as time went by, they became proficient. In January they were in the rifle pits for days on end, slowly acquiring the skills needed to hit targets from different distances and from standing, kneeling or sitting positions. Ed became an expert rifleman with great accuracy at 200 and 300 yards.

042 *Thirty Second Sketch*

043 *Artillery Range Hike*

The solders engaged in realistic field exercises where they practiced their fighting skills in faux-battles. These dry runs of military operations pitted company against company with winners and losers. Their performances were reviewed by their officers.

In the spring the company hiked into the artillery range at Spirit Creek, six miles from their home on Company B Street. It was a full-pack hike which meant they carried

all their gear with them. They camped on the range for two days and then hiked back out. There was a good deal of camaraderie among the men in their pup tents, the nights resembling a family outing with camp fires and reading by candlelight.

The exercise was meant to get the men used to field conditions but it was also an opportunity to have a look at the artillery and observe how it operated. They saw flagmen sending semaphore signals and men using field telephones.

↓ **044** *Our Tent*
← **045** *The Signaler*

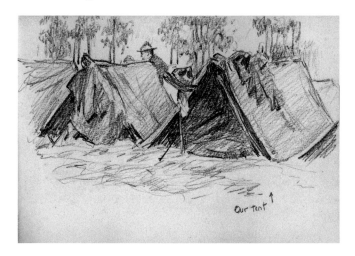

The Gun-Controll
Sketch for Comp
Augusta Ga Sept 9,1917

046 *The Gun Control*

047 *The View from My Cot by Day*

On Sundays and holidays the men did as they pleased. They slept late and lounged around camp, spent their money at the canteen or the YMCA, or went into town. As at Camp Meade, the local inhabitants embraced the soldiers. After church they were invited to meals with the local "Southern Aristocracy." There were dances and parties and Ed had time to draw whatever caught his fancy. At the end of April there was a War Bond drive at the YMCA and many of the soldiers and Augusta's citizens subscribed.

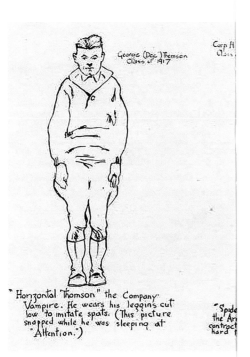

"Horizontal Thomson" the Company Vampire. He wears his leggins cut low to imitate spats. (This picture snapped while he was sleeping at "Attention.")

053 *Harold Menaugh and Doc Thompson*

things are on the mend! The Ladies of Augusta sew in the Y.M.C.A. for the soldiers.

048 *Things Are on the Mend*

BUY A BOND!

THE LAST CLIP! YOU MUST KEEP HIM SUPPLIED!

049 *Buy a Bond!*

050 *The Sunny South*

Xmas Dinner in the Army.

054 *Xmas Dinner in the Army*

Although September was warm and rainy, the Georgia winter of 1917-18 was one of the coldest on record and by December most nights were below freezing; despite their woodstoves the tents were still cold. Daily chores now included woodcutting, providing practice with the ax and saw and extra duty to those who slept late or whose uniform was not properly adjusted. On New Year's Day the men awoke to a camp covered in snow.

Thanksgiving and Christmas were holidays to remember. The whole company, nearly 200 men, sat at tables in the mess tent, which was decorated with pine boughs and holly, and were served a banquet equal to any homemade feast. They especially enjoyed the fact that their sergeants acted as their waiters.

After the holidays there was little rest as their training quickly resumed. Trench warfare included frequent close encounters with the enemy so hand-to-hand combat skills were added to their curriculum just in case the engineers had to fight one-on-one.

German soldiers were afraid of the bayonet and English instructors with combat experience taught the men how to use that fear, and their own fighting spirit to dispatch their enemy. Along with bayonet and trench knife techniques, they learned boxing and Jujitsu.

Winter is here and tents are cold places without a fire

↑ **055** *Winter is Here*

→ **056** *Captain Ryan*

God blm·e, give 'em 'ell.
English Captain in charge of bayonet-fighting.
Capt. Ryan.

0 5 7 *Six Inches of Steel for a Hun*

0 5 8 *Hand Grenade Throwing*

Later on in camp they were shown how to throw hand grenades and were trained to use the Stokes trench mortar, a simple gun with a smooth bore that could lob a bomb into the enemy's trenches. All in all, they learned everything they needed to know to be good infantrymen.

Firing a Stokes Trench Moter

059 *Firing a Stokes Trench Mortar*

Boxing in the grove!

060 *Boxing in the Grove*

As part of their training, company contested against company in games such as football and baseball. Not only was it an opportunity for competition and to keep fit, it also was a chance for men of the various companies to mingle. Boxing was not only part of their training, it was also recreation. Young men naturally wanted to know who was the strongest or toughest and pugilism was an acceptable way to do so.

"Les" Henderson lettering the Combat Wagon

061 *Lettering the Combat Wagon*

In April, 1918 things seemed to be happening. Although they continued to practice throwing hand grenades and putting up barbed wire, some officers were promoted and some left for advanced training with the division. Something was in the air, but the drilling and training continued. The men's suspicion of an upcoming move increased when they were ordered to pack all their tools and letter their combat wagon.

In early May, after 24 hours of furious preparations, Company B loaded all their equipment on a train and headed north. The men did not know exactly where they were going, but they all knew that their training was over and that their ultimate destination was France and the war.

Their time at Camps Meade and Hancock had been a great experience. There was little brutality or humiliation as the men were willing and eager to follow orders and to learn the soldier's craft. Indeed there had developed a great affection between officers and men and now that that their preparation was coming to an end, both were eager to get into the fight.

In the time Ed was in camp he filled a total of at least thirteen sketchbooks. In 310 days, in addition to everything he had to learn to be an infantry soldier, an expert rifleman and a competent combat engineer, he made a total of 262 sketches and 13 watercolors.

The training received by the 103rd Engineers had been excellent. They spent a total of ten months at Camps Meade and Hancock learning everything they needed to do their jobs and survive their perilous undertaking. With some other troops, that was not the case. Some infantry soldiers had never fired their rifles before facing the enemy and some had only a few weeks of training before combat. They were unprepared for war and their casualty rates showed it.

After his training, Ed felt confident as a soldier, as an engineer and as an artist. He had plenty of friends who looked to him as a leader. He knew how to kill a man with a rifle or a bayonet or a knife, but he wasn't sure he could. Nothing had changed his idea of war as a great romantic adventure and he was excited to see what was in store for him across the ocean.

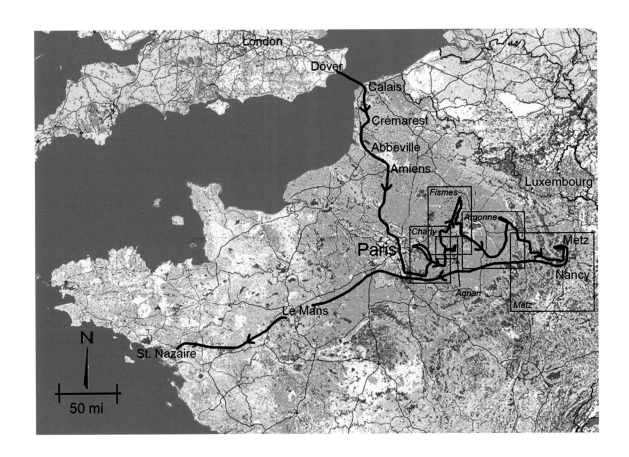

London

Dover

Calais

Crémarest

Abbeville

Amiens

Luxembourg

Fismes

Argonne

Charly

Paris

Metz

Nancy

Agnan

Metz

N

Le Mans

St. Nazaire

50 mi

GOING TO WAR
Journey to France

The entire 103rd Engineer Regiment left Camp Hancock on May 9, 1918, on their way to France; unbeknownst to their families and friends, their train passed through Philadelphia on its way to Long Island. They arrived at Camp Mills amidst the bustle of thousands of men coming and going.

The camp was a transit stop, where soldiers prepared for their trip across the Atlantic. They were there for a week, while the men's physical condition was examined, their paperwork all put in order and their equipment inspected. Additional recruits were added to bring Company B to its wartime complement of 250. Some men were lucky enough to get leave to visit New York City, and some got to say goodbye to their families, but most stayed in camp. All in all, it was a busy time of preparation and high anticipation.

On May 18 the regiment marched to a ferry, which took them up the Hudson River where they boarded the ship to France.

In April, 1918 the first phase of the German spring offensive, designed to end the war before the U.S. could affect the outcome, had ended inconclusively and the second was beginning. Both operations had the objective of forcing the British Army back to the Channel, and both failed with heavy losses on both sides.

While Ed and Don and their friends were sailing to France, the Germans began the third phase. Its goal was to take back the Chemin des Dames ridge and advance south, threatening Paris. General Ludendorff, the architect of the drive, expected the British to move troops east to reinforce the French; he would then destroy their depleted army in the west. At first the

062 *Battleship*

German Army had success, advancing to the river Marne, but once again the attack petered out with heavy casualties.

The steamer, *S. S. Metagama,* was lying in wait at Pier 58 in New York; the 103rd Signal Battalion was already on board when the engineers walked up the gangplank. She was a modern, Canadian Pacific, two-stack ocean liner that had until recently been sailing with civilian passengers from Liverpool to St. John, New Brunswick. Later that day she formed up with eleven other transports into a fast, battleship-escorted convoy taking part of the U.S. 28th Division to France.

Ed was finally off on the adventure that he had read and sketched and dreamed of for most of his life. This poem was written in an undated notebook.

Adventurers

Dreaming on the fore-deck of a soldier-laden steamer
Hastening to the wars across the endless tossing trails,
I watched a ghost fleet gather about the grey destroyers
High-pooped galleons with strange devices on their sails.

Out across the sunny sea they paced our smoky troop-ships
Going eastward with us to the low dim foreign shore,
Plunging in the head-sea til the white spray hid their fore-sails
Frobisher, Sir Francis Drake and half a hundred more.

Stained their ships from sailing where no map has ever charted,
Sails agape, and rails and spars hung with waving weeds,
Arms and armor red with rust and worn with age-long fighting
Called from phantom wanderings by news of more brave deeds.

Hardy spirits from all times to watch another venture,
Answering when the bugle blows to join the greatest game
Pennons rotted by the rains and tattered by the salt wind
Half disclosed in sun-gold mist to mark each famous name.

Faintly through the welter and the wash of tumbled water
Came the clang of armor, and the old fierce war cries rung
Wild welcome to the warriors going to the new wars.
Welcome to the proud new flag before the sunset flung.

Dark against the dim moon through the night they traveled
Shadow ships that followed us from rendezvous forlorn
Until the harbor held where they put about and vanished
Suddenly like silver haze that veils the sea at morn.

Dreaming on the fore-deck of a soldier-laden steamer
Did I dream these caravels bow-down before the breeze?
Perhaps the mists were in my eyes but this I am not doubting
Their spirit goes adventuring in us across the seas.

Once they were at sea and the fog cleared, they saw the fellow members of the convoy. The men were amazed at the number of ships spread across the ocean, but also by their weird shapes and colors. Some ships looked like fractured checkerboards and some like a wall of disjointed stripes. They were all very conspicuous but it was hard to tell which way they were headed or how far away they were. It was a camouflage scheme to confuse the German submarines. The ships were also frequently changing course as they zig-zaged across the ocean.

Their convoy consisted of nothing but fast ships and as a consequence, the threat from submarines was minimal. Although the mood was jovial and excited, no one really ever relaxed. Wherever they went, they wore their cumbersome, cork-filled life jackets, even in their cramped bunks.

The officers were all accommodated in the ship's cabins while the men were settled into tiers of tightly-packed bunks, five-high in the ship's holds. Upwards of 2,000 men sailed on the *Metagama* and when the weather was good, the decks looked like they were covered with ants.

Meals were nothing like the rather leisurely repasts in camp; all the men had to be fed in a short period of time and they frequently ate their meals standing up. The food was not as good as back at training camp and the men complained, but later, on the battlefield, they would dream of the feasts they had on board ship.

During the day there were calisthenics and lectures and daily lifeboat drills, but still a good deal of free time which the men filled with band concerts, the inevitable games of chance or by just staring out at the sea. A handful of British civilians on board organized informal performances, which were greatly appreciated. At night the ships observed a strict blackout with all hatches and portholes closed.

As the convoy approached Ireland, the battleship escort left and was replaced by a group of British torpedo boats as the threat of submarines was greater near England. Everyone was alert and watching for any sign of a periscope and one morning, as expected, something was spotted.

The troopships started evasive actions and before long there were torpedo boats dashing about and shooting at the unidentified object. Airplanes joined the fray, dropping bombs charges on the supposed undersea threat and a small dirigible floated overhead. The soldiers cheered wildly at every turn of the "battle," but no evidence of an enemy vessel was ever discovered. The lively letters written that evening were all closely censored.

←**063** *On the Rail*

064 *Something Spotted*

065 *What is It?*

Ed describes this first encounter with the enemy a bit differently. In the letter he wrote to *The Western* he stated that there were a total of three submarines, only one of which escaped. According to his "unofficial report" one was sunk by the gunners on the *Metagama* and another by a depth bomb dropped from an airplane.

On May 31, two weeks after leaving New York, Company B was once again lined up by squads on the stone quay in Liverpool. Amidst the enthusiastic welcome of their English hosts, complete with American flags and proffered cigarettes, they marched to the railway station. After greetings from pretty girls, wounded soldiers and officers of the King, they boarded the train across England.

Arriving at Dover early the next morning they were put up in a large factory for the remainder of the night. The railway station was blacked out for fear of Zeppelin raids, and they were led through the dark streets by a British officer.

By noon they were on a Channel steamer, escorted by a group of destroyers, once again dressed in their life jackets.

Later that same day, they landed in Calais and were greeted by a daring French pilot doing aerial acrobatics in a seaplane. Once safely on French soil, they marched a short distance and settled into Rest Camp # 6.

The camp was anything but restful with fifteen men crowded into the familiar conical tents which, at Camp Hancock, had housed eight. The tents were placed in pits with their vertical walls underground to keep the men safe from aerial bombs. There were no cots, the men slept on wooden floors; in the night they heard the distant rumble of cannon fire far to the east.

The Rest Camp at Calais where
no one rested —

18 cms

066 *Calais Rest Camp*

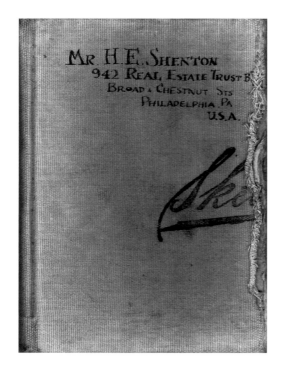

067 *Mostly Billets Sketchbook*

They remained at Calais for three days packing away their unnecessary gear including those comfort items given to them by their families. From now on, they would carry all their possessions on their backs. At the train station they boarded the infamous "40 hommes, 8 chevaux" boxcars. Built to carry 40 men or 8 horses they had one large door on the side; for the men's "comfort" the floors were covered with fresh straw; the officers rode in worn-out passenger carriages.

The weather was good as the train rolled through the farmland and small villages on the flat coastal plane of Pas de Calais and after a pleasant trip, the men arrived at Crémarest, where they stayed for the next eighteen days. While he was in Calais, Ed started sketching in a new book. After he did two sketches, he realized that it did not fit into the pocket of his pants and cut it in half.

Training in Crémarest

At the small village of Crémarest the men were initially billeted in barns and outbuildings while the officers stayed with French families in their farmhouses. When the men complained about the "dirty" conditions it was decided that they would bivouac in their pup tents in a nearby field. Evidently they had not gotten used to being constantly infested with lice, or cooties as they were affectionately called; eventually they would.

The farm-house at
our first billet in
France.

069 *Our First Billet in France*

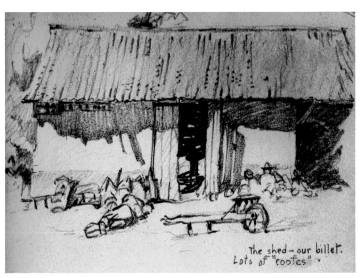

The shed – our billet.
Lots of "cooties"

070 *Cootie Shed*

Their training was continued with British officers of the Northumberland Fusiliers. Although their language was the same, the men had problems understanding the accents of their instructors. They were being fed by British cooks who underestimated the appetites of American boys, but all in all the training went well and they received the praise of their English officers.

They were introduced to the new British gas masks and became adept at putting them on in less than ten seconds. There were lectures by an English officer nicknamed Major Lethal extolling the virtues of gas when used by our side and warning of its dangers when used by the enemy.

Both sides used chemical agents of various sorts. They were usually targeted on the trenches, but anyone on the front line, or for some distance to the rear, could be gassed. The masks were effective measures against the poisonous fog and were provided for men, horses, dogs and even carrier pigeons.

071 *Gas Mask*

Cathedral of
[illegible]
Tower erected
in 1512

←**072** *Cathedral of Crémarest*

Led by an aggressive British Second Lieutenant they practiced bayonet and hand-to-hand fighting. They listened to lectures about how to conduct themselves in war and heard stories of what it was like to fight on the front lines from English veterans. Just as in Georgia, there was drilling, marching, calisthenics and games, but this time they played against their European allies. On Sunday some of the men went to church at the local cathedral.

On June 22, their period of intense infantry training was over and Company B left Crémarest. They were either deemed ready to fight or were needed at the front regardless of their fitness. Whichever was the case they marched to the station and boarded the train, but this time they were in open-topped railroad cars and could enjoy the French countryside as they headed southeast to unknown destinations.

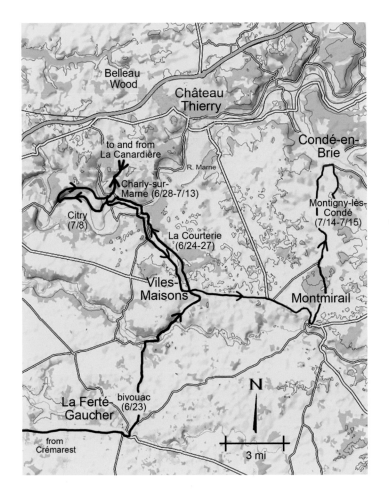

Charly-sur-Marne

After almost twenty-four hours in their open train cars, Company B finally set foot on the ground at La Ferté-Gaucher, far to the southeast of Crémarest. Most of the men were exhausted after their night ride, but they still had the enthusiasm of fresh troops going into battle for the first time. Despite their complaints about English food, they were well fed, with clean clothes, and all of their equipment was in order.

It was obvious when they left Crémarest that they were through with their training, and that they were going up to the front. They were eager for action, but that night, all they wanted was to sleep. From the train station, they marched a short way out of town and set up their pup tents.

Resting after our train-ride
thru France.

In early June the Germans attacked out of their trenches north of Chemin des Dames and moved steadily south toward the Marne. While the engineers were training at Crémarest, the enemy had reached the river at Château Thierry and continued their advance into Belleau Wood where they met the U.S. Marines. The vicious battle lasted from June 1 to the 26 but the Germans were kept from crossing the river. Defenses were needed and the 103rd Engineers were brought there to build them.

On the morning of June 24, Company B marched ten miles north to the village of La Courterie. In June 1918 there were five small farms clustered together surrounded by growing fields of waist-high wheat and corn. The barns and hay lofts would be the men's home for the next four days, while the officers were billeted in one of the farmhouses. The men practiced putting on their gas masks and were issued additional equipment. The officers sent their unneeded gear to Paris for storage and the company prepared to move closer to the front.

074 *Our Second Billet*

075 *Our Third Billet, an Old Château*

On June 28 they marched north again, crossed the Marne River at the nearly deserted town of Charly-sur-Marne and set up residence in a château near the bridge. The men bedded down in the farmworkers' rooms while the officers slept in the manor house.

On nearly every French farm there is a large manure pile in the center of the courtyard; the larger the pile, the wealthier the farmer. At first the soldiers were appalled at the stench; later the smell would remind them of the relative comfort and safety away from the front lines.

Front line of Divisional Trenches.

076 *Front Line Trenches*

During the night the Germans tried to hit the nearby bridge with artillery fire and the men moved their beds to the cellar. They got little sleep that first night and the next morning collected pieces of shrapnel as souvenirs. Within a few days, the jagged pieces of metal were so common as to be worthless, and they threw their once-precious relics away. The next day they marched north to a farm called La Canardière, the duck farm, and started digging.

They were told to gather only in small groups and shield their lights at night as enemy airplanes were looking for troop concentrations on which to direct artillery fire. There was a sense of growing excitement among the men, many of whom, Ed included, had never been farther away from home than the Jersey shore.

Marching north in the morning, building trenches and returning to the château in the afternoon would be their routine for the next two weeks. It was a lot like the training they did in Georgia except that they walked single file with a yard between to limit the number of wounded if an artillery round happened to fall among them. On their way to and from the trenches they saw big guns firing shell after shell, airplanes battling in the sky and flaming observation balloons plunging earthward, their occupants floating down under parachutes.

The engineers had learned their craft well and within a few days, the entrenchments in the woods near La Canardière were taking shape. They built dugouts with bomb-proof roofs and constructed barbed wire barricades then camouflaged their work with moss and branches. Their trenches were to remain empty unless the enemy got close.

Back in Charly-sur-Marne, the Germans were still trying to destroy the bridge, and shells were still falling near Company B's billets, but the men were getting used to the bombardment and, after the first night, when they moved their beds to the cellar, they lost little sleep. They were beginning to get a fine appreciation for the whine of the shells and the timing of their detonation. The Germans never did hit the bridge, but their explosions frequently killed fish, adding to the larder of the soldiers and the few villagers that remained in town. Despite the shelling, they had occasional parties with French soldiers, where wine and cigarettes were shared. Their conversations consisted mostly of pointing and pantomime, but their spirits were high.

On July 4 the company was awakened in the middle of the night and ordered to march to the trenches they had just constructed, as a German attack was expected. The men lined up and were issued ammunition; a dressing station for wounded was hastily set up and they marched to the front in the dark amid cannons booming from all sides and flashes in the sky lighting up the trail.

Once in the trenches, they were told that if they saw soldiers coming through the woods to wait and see if they were retreating Frenchmen or attacking Germans before opening fire. They were also ordered to hold their lines "at all cost." If the enemy overran their trenches, there was nothing to stop them marching into Paris. Meanwhile, the enemy fired shells in their direction throughout the night, but none fell close.

The moment they had been waiting for and fearing since they left Camp Hancock had come, or so they thought, but at nine in the morning, without seeing either a Frenchman or a German, they were ordered to return to the château. For nine more days they worked on the duck farm trenches and slept in the cellars next to the dung heap.

On the night of July 8 they were once again awakened and sent to a hillside overlooking the bridge at the town of Citry, two miles northwest. From their hastily-dug holes they had a view of the fighting at Château Thierry; the flare and boom of distant guns kept them entertained all night. In the morning they had breakfast from their mobile kitchen and by afternoon they were back in the comfort of their "home" by the château. So far this war was not so bad. There was lots of digging and marching and a lot of exciting things to see. They had plenty to eat and drink and regular sleep in a real bed, but in the back of their minds they knew this comfort would not last. They had not yet had their baptism of fire.

On a map far behind the front, a pin was moved and Company B drove through the night to a new destination.

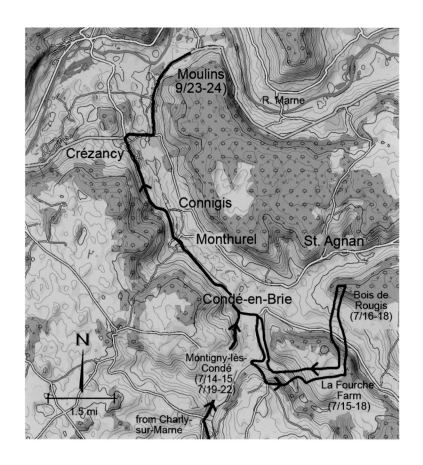

Moulins
9/23-24)

R. Marne

Crézancy

Connigis

Monthurel

St. Agnan

Condé-en-Brie

Bois de
Rougis
(7/16-18)

N

1.5 mi

Montigny-lès-
Condé
(7/14-15
7/19-22)

La Fourche
Farm
(7/15-18)

from Charly-
sur-Marne

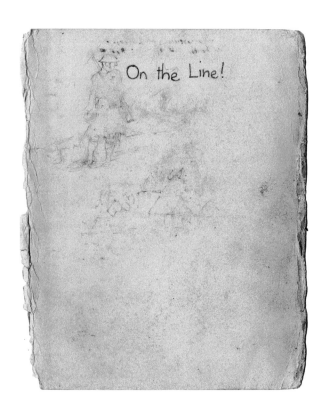

On the Line!

Saint Agnan

At Charly-sur-Marne trenches were needed and the engineers were brought in to build them. Now something else was required somewhere else and the engineers were on the move. Rumors circulated that they were headed for Paris to march in the Bastille Day parade, and with the anticipation of a holiday, they piled into trucks and took off. At Viels-Maisons they turned east instead of west; instead of Paris they were headed to another battle. It would not be the only time their plans were changed at the last minute.

←**077** *On the Line!*

078 *Camion*

At first the talk was about what they were going to do in the big city. No one in the squad had ever really seen Paris; on the train from Crémarest they had only passed through the suburbs. After they turned east, the chatter was about what they had just seen at Château Thierry. They talked for hours on the all-night ride.

The last phase of Ludendorff's spring offensive was launched on July 15. His plans to draw the British away from the west had so far come to naught, but he was less than forty miles from Paris and a breakthrough now could threaten the French capital and the British would be sure to respond. Ludendorff expected his armies to cross the Marne at many locations and drive southward, but the Allies knew the details of his plans and were strengthening their forces to meet the German push.

Ed saw the sunrise on July 14 as they were passing through the flat fields north of Condé-en-Brie. It had taken all night to move fifteen miles, but it was a short march in the warmth of early summer to the hillside village of Montigny-lès-Condé. Their billet was in a small stone barn overlooking the valley of the Marne. The rest of the day, the men settled in and dozed. Occasionally they heard the belch of a huge railroad gun firing off to the west.

079 *Possibly Montigny-lès-Condé*

During their rest the men received reports that the enemy was planning to attack the next day. That night they expected orders to build trenches or lay barbed wire but when none came, they went to bed only to be awakened by the increasingly loud sound of gunfire.

At Montigny they had a hilltop view of the battle. According to some French soldiers the German barrage was one of the fiercest since The Battle of Verdun in 1916. Later Ed wrote to *The Western* that for seven hours "it seemed as though there was nothing left on earth but noise, fire and smoke." The German shells were spreading gas in the valley below in preparation for an attack, but despite frequent alarms it never rose to their location higher on the ridge.

That afternoon all the men of Company B, even the cooks and kitchen staff, marched west to La Fourche Farm where they rested; a few slept. They were beginning to realize that they were not there to dig trenches or string wire, but to fight. At midnight they were officially designated as reserves to the 109th Infantry and as the only troops between the enemy and Paris, were ordered to hold their positions at all costs. This was the second time they heard the phrase, "at all costs" but this time there was an urgency and fear in the voices of their officers that made them think this was maybe the real thing.

Front line trench: morning. this was before the barrage began.

080 *Front Line Trench, Morning*

In the pitch dark, each holding on to the pack of the man in front, they were led through the thick woods along a poorly marked trail and took their place overlooking the German-held town of Saint-Agnan. At daybreak on July 16, Companies A and B relieved the 3rd Battalion of the 109th Infantry and occupied a series of trenches only two feet deep in front of an oak forest called the Bois de Rougis.

The day before, the 109th had been driven back from the Marne by the tidal advance of the Prussian Guards who had crossed the river at several places. At times they were surrounded and had to fight hand-to-hand to get back to their lines; many of them were killed or wounded during their retreat.

The Germans were on the north side of the valley above the town and the Americans on the south, each in plain view of the other. They were less than one thousand yards apart, well within rifle and machine gun range, and exchanged fire whenever an opportunity presented itself. All the training back in Georgia and in Crémarest on the rifle ranges now became very important.

"Where'd that un go?"

081 *Where'd That Un Go?*

Later in the morning artillery shells started to fall in front of the men in their shallow trenches. At first they landed a hundred yards away and were louder than anything they had heard at Charly. At thirty yards the shells left a ringing in the ears and as the explosions came closer, the men were deafened by the concussions.

They were crouched down with their faces in the bottom of the trench when the barrage hit. The Germans had zeroed in on their location and poured in fire for what seemed like an eternity. The bombardment lasted more than an hour; one man from Company B was killed and ten were wounded; all had now gone through their initiation of combat.

Front line trench
evening.

Shell-shocked and
exhausted men waiting
for darkness to be taken
out.

082 *Front Line Trench, Evening*

During a lull in the shelling, the 109th Infantry, now regrouped from their retreat of the day before, charged from the woods, through Company B's trenches and into the wheat field at the base of the hill, all under intense fire, and re-took Saint-Agnan. The casualties were high and several of the wounded soldiers were rescued by engineers. After an hour the shellfire began to increase again and the decision was made to move the men from the shallow trenches back to the cover of Bois de Rougis.

One by one they ran to the woods under fire. They dug individual holes and small trenches and stayed in them for the next two days, all the while under a rain of high explosives, shrapnel and splinters from shattered trees. An ever increasing number of wounded engineers were evacuated back to a hospital dugout in the rear. Despite the nearly constant enemy fire, the cooks were able to provide the men with coffee and one hot meal.

Thanks to the 109th Infantry, the French Chasseurs Alpins and the 103rd Engineers the farthest advance of the German Army was Saint-Agnan. Company B was holding its part of the line at the enemy's deepest penetration across the Marne. Without any combat experience, the engineers had done their job, this time as fighting soldiers rather than trench builders.

At 5:00 in the afternoon of July 18 the men began to leave
Bois de Rougis and return to La Fourche Farm. Company B
had been decimated in their first battle, but performed their
duties without faltering. What was left of the company arrived
at 8:00 that night and bivouacked in the woods.

Company B left New York with 250 men, but after the
battle there were only 185 left. Five men were killed in the
trenches above the wheat field or in the woods. Their stand
against the enemy at Saint-Agnan resulted in the largest
number of casualties of any of their battles. Everyone had
a friend who was no longer there; Ed was acquainted with
at least twelve of the casualties.

As a consequence of their stand against the advancing
German army, General Pershing gave the 28th Division
the nickname "Iron Division."

This is home.

083 *This is Home*

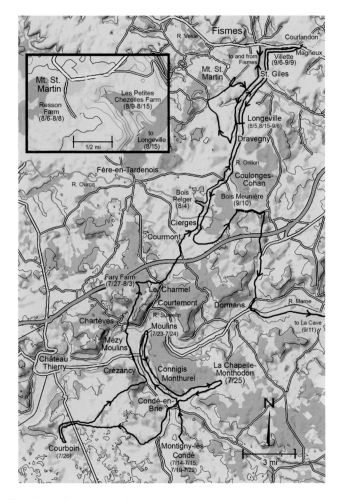

Fismes

The next day the still-exhausted men marched back to Montigny-lès-Condé and stayed in the village for the next two days. They rested and checked their equipment and replaced what had been lost or destroyed.

With far fewer mouths to feed, there was plenty of food for breakfast. At the morning roll call Fred Quimby, Freddie Street and Doc Thompson and many of the men Ed had known at Camps Meade and Hancock were missing.

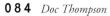

084 *Doc Thompson*

085 *Freddie Street*

086 *Street in a Ruined Town*

Ed sat looking out over the valley where he had seen the German shells bursting a few days earlier. It was quiet now as the enemy had retreated north to the Ourcq River. He was not thinking of Sir Nigel or The White Company; the idea of a noble crusade was far from his mind. He was thinking of his friends and of the terrors of the shallow trenches and of the woods. He picked up his sketchbook and began to draw.

The German army had planned for the possibility of retreat and had fortified a line of defense on the Ourcq. They were still fighting a stiff delaying action and men on both sides were still dying. As the 111th and 112th Infantry, fellow regiments in the 28th Division, pushed north the 103rd Engineers followed in their wake.

Early on the morning of July 22, Company B left the comfort of their village billets at Montigny-lès-Condé and marched down into the valley of the Surmelin. What little time Ed had to mourn the loss of his friends was over. The war was going on and, like it or not, he was still a part of it. They entered towns shelled by the Germans during the offensive of July 15, and by the Allies three days later. The roads through Monthurel and Connigis were nearly impassable and the fields were full of the wastage of battle: shell holes, discarded supplies, ruined equipment, and dead soldiers.

My home

The Fourth Billet. About the most ancient village that we have struck in France.

Burying Detail

← **087** *Fourth Billet*

↑ **088** *Burying Detail*

Their destination for the day had been Courtemont but when the town was found to be contaminated by gas, it was decided that they should stay in Moulins instead. They were still south of the Marne and at the end of the day they were able to shelter in the basements of houses mostly untouched by the fighting.

The next two days were spent in cellars in Moulins. They only worked at night as in the light they were easy targets for enemy guns. They spent the darkness filling shell holes on the river road and burying the dead. It was good to have something to do to put the horror of Bois de Rougis behind them.

"B Company
Kitchen.

On July 25 the men were told they were going away from the fighting for a rest, but after two days of marching, their orders were countermanded and they headed back to the battle once again.

They crossed the Marne on a pontoon bridge near Chartèves at noon on July 27 and passed through towns even more devastated than those south of the river. Marching all day in the rain through a broken land filled with the odor of death did little to raise their morale. They spent the rainy night on the ground in a wood that smelled of gas and dead horses. One of their few comforts was their rolling kitchen, and the cooks who provided them with hot meals.

←**089** *"B" Company Kitchen*

The next day the men dug in at Fary Farm near La Charmel where they stayed in dugouts for the next week. Some men spent the day cutting stakes in a local forest while the others filled shell holes and erected defensive wire at night under shellfire.

Ever since they crossed the Marne they had been passing from untouched fields of wheat and red poppies into a stale land, spoiled by war, where the foul evidence of battle was everywhere: shattered trees, wrecked guns and demolished wagons; bloody dressings and broken bayonets; photos, letters and bibles; and bodies, everywhere bodies. As the engineers often arrived days after the battle, the corpses were black and bloated.

090 *Dead Germans in a Wheat Field*

Where the Doughboys
"Dug-in" beside the Soissons-
Fismes-Reims Railroad

Along the Vesle

091 *Along the Vesle*

In early August the enemy gave up their defensive positions on the Ourcq River and swiftly moved north, the infantry in pursuit and the engineers following closely behind. The regiment advanced nearly ten miles in the next two days passing through Courmont, Cierges, Coulonges-Cohan and Dravegny. They finally stopped at the small village of Longeville where they camped in the nearby woods to be out of sight. There was little enemy fire and the villages they passed through were mostly undamaged; some civilians were still in residence.

The German's next line of resistance was the Vesle River. They had occupied the town of Fismes since the spring and now were awaiting an attack.

To locate the enemy lines, the Pennsylvanians of the 110th and 112th Infantry sent scouting parties to approach the town from the south. The Germans were on the north side of a railroad embankment near the river; the doughboys dug into the opposite bank and for several nights, listened to the enemy only few yards away.

German shells bursting in a Town

The Hun Shelling an American battery of 75's

The Germans decided not to hold Fismes, but retreated across the river, leaving a rear guard to make the Americans pay dearly. On August 4, after a long day of house-to-house fighting and a barrage that further wrecked the town, the 112th Infantry was in control of the ruins.

The next day, Ed Shenton and Company B marched from Longeville, arriving at the high ground near Mont-Saint-Martin at dawn to find Fismes being heavily shelled. They retreated quickly to a nearby wood to avoid enemy fire.

← **092** *German Shells Bursting in a Town*
↑ **093** *The Hun Shelling an American Battery of 75's*

From the woods at Mont-Saint-Martin they moved a short distance to nearby Resson Farm and dug in. For two days they cleared the roads and improved their dugouts, but there was a nearby artillery battery which drew German fire and after a large shell hit a building at the farm, killing several men, it was decided that they should move again.

Home No 10

The following day
No 11
Aug 10

094 *Homes No. 10 and 11 at Resson Farm and Les Petites Chezelles Farm*

After Resson they set up camp at Les Petites Chezelles Farm. On the L'Orillon River, the location was more protected and the men dug their new homes once again.

The upper drawing is from Resson Farm and shows Ed's home after two days of improvements. The lower is of their hastily constructed dugout at Les Petites Chezelles Farm the next day.

The French general in charge of the area in and around Fismes deemed the town of Fismette, on the north bank of the Vesle, essential to the success of the operation and ordered troops to capture it. The infantry needed foot bridges to bring in soldiers, a wagon bridge for food and ammunition, and a bridge for ambulances to evacuate the wounded and it was the job of the engineers to build them.

The Vesle was too wide and deep to ford, but not wide enough to pose a major barrier and small footbridges sufficed to move troops across. The main problem was that the river was under constant observation and enemy fire.

At Chezelles Farm the engineers loaded timbers onto trucks, drove them into town at night and carried them through the streets on their shoulders. If the enemy lit up the darkness with a flare, they had to stand still to avoid being seen and shot at; one man was killed doing this work.

Hasty foot-bridge across
the Vesle above Fismes

E.S.

↑ **095** *Hasty Footbridge*

→ **096** *Engineer Dugout*

To unload the trucks and build the bridges, a squad
of sixteen men was needed in Fismes and an officer was
sent to find a safe place for them to stay. Above ground,
nowhere in the town was immune from enemy fire, but
they found a suitable cellar with an arched opening for
their command post.

Engineer dug-out

Engineer P.C. in Fismes

097 *Engineers' P. C. in Fismes*

This poem by Charles Ruff, one of the West Philly High fifteen who joined with Ed, is the best description of what the men of Company B experienced in Fismes:

We saw it first at night, when every house
Roofless, shell-shattered, naked to the sky
Was lit by gleam of Very light
Which falling, made the gliding shadows fly.

We saw whole streets where wine shop, store and home
Blazed on for days, unquenched by mortal man
We stumbled over nests of tinkly wire
Where once its webbed communications ran.

Sniped at, we raced close, with beating heart
We skulked among the ruins like a thief,
We lay in cellars vainly fighting flies
And praying for our hour of relief.

We heard the drone of bullets in the air,
The heart-contracting whine and crash of shell,
The fall of tott'ring walls; in street and yard
We marked the corpses rotting where they fell.

Such was the town; and then the Bosche fell back,
Fresh troops came up, and wagons filled the street.
We saw unknowing strangers, unconcerned,
Pass one time deadly points with careless feet.

So swift the change we're amazed to see
Men walk the street unharmed while it was light.
Such boldness seemed like dreadful sacrilege
To us, the furtive dodgers of the night.

Since the enemy held the high ground, he could see everything
that was going on, both in Fismes and for several miles south
of the river. The town itself was within range of all the weapons
in the Germans' arsenal: rifles, machine guns, cannons, mortars,
and they used every one. They had occupied the town long
enough to know every corner and alleyway by heart and could
put a shell or a bullet anywhere they wanted. Some snipers were
even adept at ricocheting rifle bullets off the stone buildings
to kill around a corner. Moving around the town during the
day was a tricky and dangerous business. The men ducked into
alleyways and sheltered behind buildings until they made a dash
from one place to another.

The City Hall when Jerry Finished the prelude

the Town Hall a week later

← **098** *The City Hall after Jerry Finished the Prelude*
↑ **099** *The Town Hall a Week Later*

A favorite target for German fire was the city hall. It had been their headquarters when they occupied the town and they now seemed intent on demolishing it completely. Ed drew the ruin of the building twice, one week apart showing the increased damage.

On the front line communication between units was difficult. As soon as telephone wire was laid, it was destroyed by shellfire. The few radios that were in use at the time were fragile and seldom worked in the heat of battle so runners were used to send messages. They worked in pairs so if one was wounded, the other could get the message through. It was one of the most dangerous – and adventurous – of jobs. A runner had to be fast, agile and know his way around; he had to avoid shellfire, and dodge bullets. Runners were frequently killed, but none hesitated when called upon to do their duty. Runners taking messages either between front line units or to the rear had the most casualties while those communicating behind the lines had the least.

100 *Runners in Fismes*

GAS

101 *Gas*

All the bridge work was done at night, but despite the darkness, the enemy gunners knew where the engineers were working, and had guns zeroed in on their locations. The men did their work steadily under constant fire from artillery, machine guns, and rifles and casualties were high. The infantry fought for nearly a month in Fismette with the engineers constantly building and rebuilding the bridges.

On August 12 they were finishing up the ambulance bridge. The decking planks had to be nailed in place, but any noise would bring machine gun fire. The men were equipped with hammers and proceeded to nail down all the planks at once creating a loud racket. In less than a minute, shellfire hit near the bridge covering the men with mud and water, and the machine gun bullets began to fly, but by then the work was complete. The bridge was finished and no one was wounded.

While conditions in Fismes were difficult and dangerous, those back at Les Petites Chezelles Farm were little better. Despite their distance from the enemy, they still received their share of attention from the German guns firing at the nearby artillery battery. On August 13 shells killed several horses and gassed the battery on the hill above the farm. The mustard gas rolled down into the dugouts where the engineers were sleeping. Despite efforts to fan out the trenches with paddles, fifteen men were overcome and had to be evacuated to the hospital.

While one platoon of Company B was in Fismes, the others at the farm prepared defensive positions in case the enemy broke through. They erected camouflage fences along the road, dug trenches and strung barbed wire from Dravegny to Saint-Gilles, all, of course, under frequent artillery fire.

On August 15 the company moved south to Longeville where they were farther from the front and less likely to be shelled. Men were still regularly rotated in and out of Fismes, repairing bridges and keeping the roads open in the heat of the battle, but for the most part the work behind the front was routine. The area had become crowded, with men and equipment halfway back to the Marne, waiting for a breakthrough so they could move north, but the infantry was stalled in Fismette.

There was a field hospital near Longeville where the men scrounged for new clothes, some with holes and bloodstains. Even if they couldn't properly bathe, the clothes, which were cleaner than those they had been wearing for a month, made them feel marginally more civilized.

102 *Camouflage on a Road*

Sunday afternoon, the 'reading room' attached to the Dug-out.

103 *The Reading Room*

Back in Fismes, the engineers stayed in their cellar during the day, venturing out at night to do their work. The town was deserted and most of its buildings in ruins, but the engineers' accommodations appear to have been rather commodious. The thick walls kept out the noise of the fighting and the men were able to relax, read and write letters home. When there was no night work, there was singing and poker games. The stress of being under fire was periodically relieved by rest at Longeville. During the stalemate at Fismette, there was even time for some men to be taken back from the front for delousing, a bath and to hear a band.

Despite the great risk, some of the men at Fismes went out very carefully during the day, creeping and dodging to avoid snipers. The populace had evacuated the town in a hurry, leaving behind most of the everyday amenities that the soldiers craved. Ed went on some of these daytime forays and back in the cellar, drew what he had seen. Drawing was his way of coming to grips with all the dirt, stench, vermin and horror of the war.

"Mendy" finds a magazine in a wrecked shop.

104 *Mendy Finds a Magazine*

Bridge across the Vesle below
Magneaux. Sept 7-8 1918

105 *Bridge Across the Vesle Below Magneaux*

On September 4, exactly one month after the 112th pushed the enemy out of Fismes, the German Army began to withdraw its troops and artillery to make a stand farther north. They retreated to the Aisne River where they dug in and stayed for the rest of the war. The enemy's hasty withdrawal from the Vesle brought about a rapid pursuit.

The traffic jam on the roads was broken and large numbers of troops and artillery pieces and huge amounts of ammunition and supplies had to cross the river in a short time. Bridges were needed for soldiers both coming from and going into battle and the engineers went back to work in earnest.

Company B built and repaired wagon bridges east of Fismes, in Villette, Magneux and Courlandon to accommodate the tremendous volume of traffic headed to the front. Despite their retreat, the enemy was still able to shell the bridges and men were being killed, gassed and injured; they could still only do their work at night.

The Germans crudely wired bunches of grenades on some of the damaged bridges, which were deftly removed before they were repaired. Once the bridges were safe, the engineers directed traffic: fresh French troops moving north into battle and weary Americans headed south for a rest.

On September 7 Company B moved from Longeville to Villette where they stayed in the caves and tunnels of a limestone quarry. It is ironic that the closer they got to the front, the safer their shelter. More men were injured in the dugouts at Longeville and Les Petites Chezelles than in either the cellars of Fismes or the caves of Villette.

On the morning of September 9 the 103rd was relieved and left the battlefield. Fismes had been a month-long ordeal that none of them would ever forget.

During the first week of September the 103rd Engineers built or repaired a total of fourteen bridges in the vicinity of Fismes. Some were small footbridges for troops, but others were large portable bridges, sturdy enough for the bigger artillery pieces along with the ammunition and ration trucks that followed.

In all the work they did to support the infantrymen, the engineers acquitted themselves honorably. Although they did not fight the enemy, they withstood the same continuous shelling as the infantry. When the barrage began, they could not seek shelter in a trench, but had to continue their work in the open.

In the Cave at Villette

"Fall Out on the Right!" Going out of the Marne Sector Sept 9 1918

After the war, Ed wrote this poem about his experiences in Fismes.

108 *Doughboy*

*Which of you have forgotten
The road that winds to Fismes
With infantry plodding the edges
The center for guns and teams?*

*While over the hills in the twilight
The first barrage begins
And the Mower comes out with his baskets
To gather the fruit for his bins*

*The gas drifts down Death Valley
On the edges of a wandering breeze
And the trailing signal rockets
Climb slowly above the trees*

*The drum-fire flares are beating
An aurora across the skies
And a Very light shakes the darkness
To a frightened glare and dies*

*While under the shade of your helmet
You drag on a cigarette….
Which of you have forgotten?
Which of you would forget?*

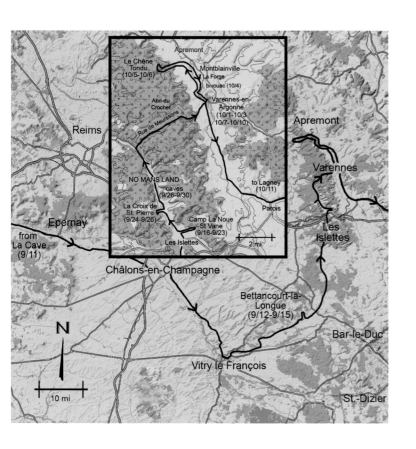

Meuse-Argonne

Once again they marched away from the fighting, first to Longeville and then farther south. They rested one day along the route, got new clothes, then continued to the Marne, where they were loaded into trucks for a journey far from the battle still raging north of the Vesle. They had been in combat, under fire, on or near the front lines nearly every day for the last two months. Nobody thought they were done with the war, but everyone was ready for a long rest.

"Spuds" Rabbit and "Offs" at Bettancourt

The first Sunday behind the lines. Bettancourt

↑ **109** *Rabbits and Offs*

→ **110** *First Sunday Behind the Lines*

At noon on September 12 they arrived at Bettancourt-la-Longue and spent the next few days cleaning up, repairing their gear and best of all, eating, drinking and sleeping. For the first time in many weeks they relaxed and enjoyed fresh meat and eggs. September 15 was the first Sunday they had spent out of the front lines since they stepped off the train on June 28; the next day they headed back to battle.

For the first time in the war the American Army was acting independently and was about to begin an attack in the Argonne Forest with the goal of capturing the strategically important railroad yards on the Meuse River, only six miles from the German border. The huge offensive would involve over one million men and require supplies at an unprecedented rate.

The Argonne was a relatively quiet sector with many trenches that had been in place since the Germans' first drive stalled in September of 1914, and the enemy was not expecting an attack through the dense forest.

On September 16 the engineers were trucked north to the village of Les Islettes then marched down a narrow muddy path to the barracks that would be their home for the next week. Infantry troops, artillery and supplies were concealed in the nearby woods and the soldiers were warned not to let themselves be seen lest they ruin the surprise of the attack scheduled for September 26. They readied their equipment and loaded their wagons and trucks in preparation for the upcoming battle, all in the secrecy of the forest. On the night of the 23rd they marched to a dense wood near a place called La Croix de St. Pierre where they dug in. On the 24th and 25th the men repaired roads and showed the infantrymen the best way to cut through barbed wire barriers.

They prepared for the artillery attack by cutting the trees hidding the cannons nearly through and holding them up with wires. At 5:30 in the morning the trees were pulled down and the cannonade started. As the barrage rolled on, the infantry advanced behind it. They followed the exploding shells and attacked the Germans who were still hunkered down in their dugouts. As the battle began, Company B moved forward to trenches only a short distance behind the front line.

111 *Gas and Wire*

112 *American Ambulance*

Just after the last wave of soldiers passed their trenches, the engineering officers assessed the situation and called for the men to move up and start repairing the main road. What they discovered was that the area for 1000 yards on either side of the trenches had been shelled for the last four years, and there was no longer any road to repair. It was the No-Man's-Land that they had heard of, but this was the first time they had seen it… and they had to quickly put a road across it.

That morning, as the smell of the artillery still hung in the air, the engineers filled shell holes, cleared tangles of barbed wire and bridged dilapidated trenches. The new road was built around and between huge mine craters, some of which were thirty feet deep. At times the men came across the bones of soldiers who had died years earlier.

To the north of No-Man's-Land the engineers found a narrow-gage railway, used its bed for their new road and finally connected it to the old main route. The shellfire from the retreating German cannons was bothersome at first, but died down as the guns retreated north. By the September 27 traffic was moving and by the 28th it was full of ambulances, ration wagons and artillery moving forward, all chaotically mixed with troops marching to and from the front.

113 *Ration Wagon*

114 *French Howitzer*

There was always an enthusiasm for repairing roads because it allowed the rolling kitchen and the ration wagon to follow the men. A passable road meant everyone would be fed, engineers included.

The repair and improvement of the road to its junction with the route to Varennes was more of a job than the 103rd Engineers could handle on their own so they were joined by several other units, including companies of black soldiers. The men worked day and night digging ditches for drainage and paving the road with logs. The corduroy highway was bumpy, but still passable after five days of rain.

Where the road still existed, it was blocked by anti-tank mines or unexploded airplane bombs, which had to be removed. The Germans also booby trapped their abandoned dugouts with turtle-shaped grenades. Fortunately the troops were aware of these devices and no one was injured.

On October 1 Company B moved from the area north of La Croix de St. Pierre to the town of Varennes-en-Argonne where they once again repaired the main road. The area had been occupied for the last four years, but was recaptured on the first day of the battle after heavy shelling.

"Vell, I midt pe deadt"

+N. 27

Nearby in the forest at a place called Abri du Crochet the Germans had built a rest area with faux beer gardens and peaked-roofed chalets. There was a swimming pool, a bowling alley and a library which included works in German by Arthur Conan Doyle (perhaps there was a well-read copy of *Sir Nigel* or *The White Company* among them), all to remind exhausted troops of home and take their minds off the war. The area was overrun so quickly by the 77th Division that laundered uniforms still hung in closets, and freshly-cooked meals sat uneaten on tables.

At this point in the battle, German prisoners were moving south in large numbers. Not only did the American soldiers see a defeated enemy, but also a walking souvenir shop. They routinely cut the buttons from the coats of the prisoners as they were marched to the rear. The captives displayed little resistance because for them the war was over, and they had survived.

←**115** *Prisoner of War*

After their first spectacular breakthrough, the Americans bogged down. Fighting from reinforced concrete bunkers the enemy had been able to slow their advance to a crawl and casualties were growing steadily. Once again the engineers were assigned as reserve, this time for the 111th Infantry. On October 4 they marched north of Varennes, where they spent the day in trenches without incident, but the real battle was elsewhere and as the sun set, they moved westward toward the fight.

Company B marched through the night and arrived at the foot of Le Chêne Tondu in the dark. The Germans had placed their artillery on the steep ridge and were determined to hold it regardless of their losses, but the 111th had a similar determination to drive them out.

The engineers dug in on the reverse slope. Conventional artillery fire went over their heads, but in the middle of the night, mortar bombs began to fall into the shallow trenches. Memories of Bois de Rougis flashed through their minds. Five men were killed and as many wounded, and, like Saint-Agnan, their evacuation was difficult. In the morning they moved to the top of the hill, protected by a sunken road.

116 *Doughboys Bringing Back Wounded*

Baby Tanks at Varennes.

117 *Baby Tanks at Varennes*

The ridge was covered with dense forest, through which the French had cut long, straight roads for logging and fire fighting. The German machine guns fired down these lanes preventing anyone from crossing. If the engineers were called on to relieve the infantry, they would have to cross these deadly paths, but fortunately, the men of the 111th were able to outflank the machine guns and push the enemy back before the engineers had to make their dash. Many medals were awarded in the fight for Le Chêne Tondu, but many men also died in the woods. On October 6 the infantry moved on and Company B was left behind to bury the dead and improve the sunken road.

In this phase of the war, the use of tanks was commonplace. Due to the dense forest and frequent ravines, they were seldom effective in the Argonne and were of no help at Le Chêne Tondu. Most broke down or were damaged during the fighting and were hauled to a repair park in Varennes.

German "Feldbahnhof" at La Forge Ferme

118   *Feldbahnhof*

On October 7 Company B returned to Varennes where they removed explosives from a German dugout, repaired roads and a narrow gauge railway, and camouflaged the main route to Montblainville. They were in Varennes for three more days until they moved once again to the rear.

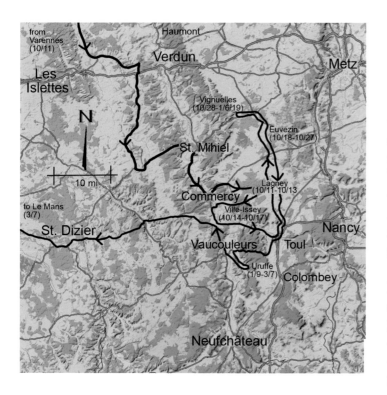

Metz

Company B's time in the small town of Lagney and later at Ville-Issey was like paradise. They were one hundred miles from the front and arrived in the middle of the grape harvest. There was fresh fruit everywhere, and the soldiers helped with the winemaking. They bathed, their clothes were "de-cooty-ized," and they drank plenty of wine, but after a week of recuperation, and two baths, they were once again headed for their next appointment with the war.

A month earlier the American Expeditionary Forces and French troops, both commanded by General Pershing, had swept the enemy from a southward bulge which the Germans had occupied for four years. The battle of Saint-Mihiel went well for the allies and now from that new front line, the Doughboys were going to attack again to push the enemy back toward Metz.

119 *Vigneulles*

120 *Vigneulles Ruins*

On October 17 Company B moved by truck to the small village of Euvezin, east of Saint-Mihiel, where they were to act as relief infantry as well as combat engineers for the attack on Metz. On their way north, they passed through French villages that had been flattened in the recent battle, and a No-Man's-Land near the old front line. Occasionally a long range shell burst close by, but when they reached Euvezin, the front was five miles away and there was little enemy activity.

Once settled they began repairing and surveying roads, building dugouts, inspecting bridges, stringing barbed wire, and salvaging camouflage material, all in preparation for the upcoming offensive. On October 28 they moved west to Vigneulles-lès-Hattonchâtel, where they were quartered in a barracks west of the town. In their rapid retreat from the Saint-Mihiel salient, the Germans had left behind all manner of supplies, both for war and for their own comfort and the American soldiers were comfortably billeted in their enemies' former lodging.

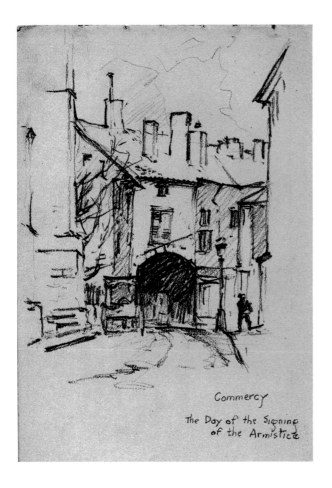

Commercy

The Day of the Signing
of the Armistice

The weather had been fair but cool in the first few days of November, and the work on the flat roads between fields of recently harvested wheat was pleasant with blue skies and puffy clouds. The war seemed a world away, but the veterans knew better and on November 10 they moved closer to the front. Their duties were to cut through the enemy wire for the next day's attack, and to act once again as infantry reserve, this time for the 109th. The attack began in the early hours of November 11. German shells fell heavily on the soldiers concentrated near the town of Haumont, killing several men in the last minutes of the war. The American attack had failed to reach the enemy wire when, at 11:00 am, all fell silent. The Armistice had taken effect; the intense German artillery barrage stopped; unarmed German troops came across the line to exchange cigarettes and souvenirs; the war was over.

The battle of the Meuse-Argonne had lasted forty seven days; the 26,000 men killed in those seven weeks was more than in any battle fought by American soldiers before or since.

← **121** *Armistice at Commercy*

After the Armistice German soldiers were no longer a threat, but they were still a curiosity. They were allowed to go home and to keep their small arms, but if they did not leave occupied territories in two weeks, they would become prisoners of war.

Although the German General Staff was not required to admit defeat by surrendering, their army was everywhere retreating in the face of an overwhelming allied onslaught. German ports had been blockaded for four years and the people were starving. With their economy in ruins and the nation in the throes of revolution, the decision was made by a new government to stop fighting. Ludendorff had lost his gamble that he could win the war before U.S. troops arrived.

On November 10, the day after he abdicated, Kaiser Wilhelm II, then a private citizen, crossed the border from Belgium into the neutral Netherlands and spent the rest of his life in exile. He bought a small estate near the town of Doorn where he let out his pent-up frustration by cutting down the estate's trees; he became known locally as the "woodchopper of Doorn." When he died in 1941 swastikas were displayed at his funeral.

Giving the Jerrys a Once Over after the Armistice American Outpost above Haumont, November 12 1918

122 *Germans at Haumont*

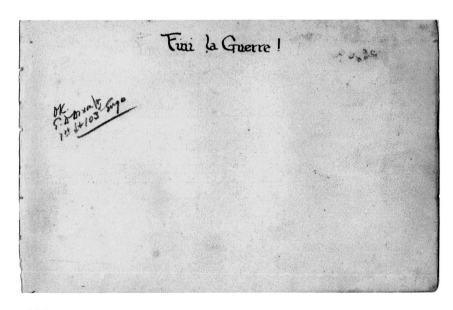

123 *Fini la Guerre!*

FINI LA GUERRE!

After the last shots of the war had been fired, Company B remained in the vicinity of Vigneulles where they rested and repaired their equipment. After a week the men began to truly relax, having finally realized that they had fought their last battle. There was no longer the threat of being blown to pieces by a bursting shell or cut in half by machine gun bullets. The marching to and from the sound of the fighting was over, as were the flashes of illumination in the dark and the constant din of artillery shells. They could bathe and eat and sleep without the knowledge that soon their rest would be interrupted and they would once again be called upon to build a bridge or repair a road; or to dig a trench or bury a dead soldier. They would never again have to aim their rifle at an enemy or cower in a hole in the ground. They were sad for their friends who had left them but were relieved that they had survived.

The army wanted to move rapidly north to fill the vacuum left by the retreating Germans so the engineers went back to work clearing rubble from the roads and filling shell holes. They removed collapsed houses near what once was the front line and disassembled the obstacles that both they and the enemy had constructed to keep the other at bay.

In the course of the war, the Germans made and sowed over three million anti-tank mines, often in dense arrays only a few feet apart. As a condition of the Armistice, they were required to reveal their location and assist in their neutralization. Some were as simple as artillery shells buried nose upward and others were wooden boxes filled with explosives, buried in shallow holes. Now that the fighting was over and civilians were returning to their farms, these had to be removed. On November 20 Company E was clearing mines somewhere in the area when one of them exploded and five men, including Don Shenton, were killed.

We will never know if Ed and Don spent any time together after the Armistice. The regiment was spread out over a large area and although they were still officially billeted in Vigneulles, various companies, squads and platoons were working in different towns.

Throughout their lives the brothers had been close and Ed must have been devastated by Don's death. Don had cared for him when he was bedridden and was his "co-driver" for the imagined 55th St. Hillclimbs in their fantasy Simplex "Red Devil." They worked side by side on *The Western* and enlisted together at the Philadelphia armory. Although in France they were separated much of the time, they saw each other when they could.

Ed had little time to mourn. The army was anxious to move into Luxembourg and the roads had to be repaired, but by the middle of December, Company B was back in its barracks. Although Ed had the opportunity to reflect on his brother's death, no drawings or writings have been found that show his grief and his son Ned never heard of his father speak of Don's death.

By Christmas most of their work was done and their time was taken up with close-order drill, training on the rifle range, courses of one kind or another and guard duty. The men were now clean, well fed and rested, but they were getting bored. On Sundays some of the men attended local religious services and Ed took the opportunity to sketch the interior of the church in the nearby town of Hattonchâtel.

124 *Hattonchâtel Church*

The oldest inhabitant
The Rat Hunter.

Even though the fighting had stopped more than a month before, they were still in a land devastated by four years of war. Like so many towns, Vigneulles was shattered; its remaining citizens scratching for a living. Roads were jammed with people day and night, going back to their homes or looking for lost relatives. In many villages, the harvest had been interrupted and the returning residents needed food from elsewhere to keep from starving; vermin were everywhere. Like their neighbors, those soldiers who remained over Christmas had to have their feast brought up from those areas of France not touched by the fighting.

During the holidays the men of the 28th Division were issued red keystone patches to wear on their left shoulders representing the Keystone State and two golden chevrons for their left sleeves, each chevron indicating six months in a combat zone. These accoutrements garnered respect from fellow soldiers as the Pennsylvanians moved into the rear areas.

←**125** *The Rat Hunter*

"Well, we did it, what?" Φ

126 *Keystones*

127 *Chevrons*

This is Old Joe. He spends his time looking for washings for his wife to do. She is '97.

↑ **128** *Old Joe*
↗ **129** *Uruffe Washerwoman*

From 14 to 74, they all wash clothes. —
Uruffe

On January 6, 1919 the men marched three days to Uruffe, a village of 400 inhabitants far from the front lines, and little touched by the war. It was part of the pipeline for thousands of soldiers on their way home and was crowded with Americans. The men repaired the old Roman roads which had withstood traffic for hundreds of years; the excess wear of thousands of army trucks coming and going had torn them apart.

130 *Rail Yards at Commercy*

The people of Uruffe were thankful for the town full
of soldiers as they had well-paid employment washing their
clothes, and the men were thankful to have clean uniforms.

While in Uruffe, Ed visited Commercy to the north and
Neufchâteau to the south and drew whatever caught his eye.
Interesting things were going on wherever he went and
he wanted to capture everything he could.

131 *Mongolian at Neufchâteau*

There was training on the rifle range and the usual entertainments, including some horse shows, but there was also ample free time. Generous leave was granted and the men traveled near and far. Some visited the mountain town of Le Mont-Dore, west of Lyon where they enjoyed the hot mineral baths; Ed went for a week of skiing in Chamonix. This poem was found in a notebook written after he returned to the U.S.

Chamonix

Seven days in Chamonix
White bread and cream
White sheets enfolding me
A pillow for my head
And the Alps to shut away
The roar of guns; the dead

Seven days in Chamonix
Skiing in the sun
High in through the dark
Stars shining unfeelingly
And not a Very light
Or the red breath of the howitzer
To beat against the night

Seven days in Chamonix
Fragments of dreams
Linked into memories
And now I'm going back
And the train winds down from quiet heights
To dugouts, mud, hard tack.

French Bombing
Machine
(Night Bomber)
Colombey

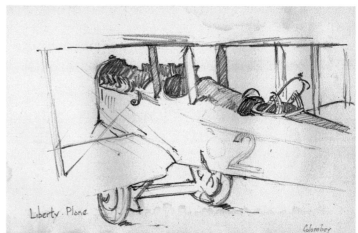

Liberty. Plane

Colombey

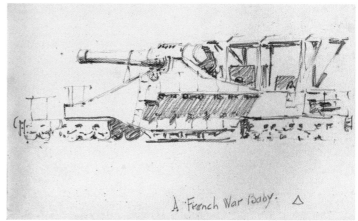

A French War Baby. △

↗ **132** *Liberty Plane*
↑ **133** *Night Bomber*
↘ **134** *Railway Gun*

In early March General Pershing reviewed the entire 28th
Division in a large field just west of Colombey-les-Belles.
The troops camped for several days and engaged in football
games with other units of the division. It was like a scout
jamboree or a huge family get-together. There was plenty
to see, including a nearby airfield, and Ed had many subjects
for his pencil.

Infantry!

Doughboy Guard.
"Hell if thu Infantry....

Artillery.

Well, I guess if it weren't for a barrage
or two....

Engineers

Maybe we didn't win this war but ve strung
enough wire for the next five"

↑ **135** *Infantry*

↗ **136** *Artillery*

↗ **137** *Engineer*

With no enemy to fight, no roads to repair or bridges to build, the men had time to talk, and drink and one of their favorite topics at Colombey was who won the war. Each group – infantry, artillery, engineers, cooks, stevedores, even stable boys – had their opinion and often voiced it loudly and defended

Stevedores

"Don' fo'get me, Boss! Ah, winned some ob dis heah wah !"
No gourd.

The Cook.

"It's not I wot speaks. Napoleon, hisself said a Army travels on it's belly . . . ."

the Stable-Rat

"If you wanta know who win thu war come an' ask me ol' mule —"

their premise physically. The conflict was becoming so widespread that the army issued a ban on discussing who exactly was responsible for defeating the enemy.

138 *Stevedore*
139 *Cook*
140 *Stable Rat*

141 *40 Hommes et 8 Chevaux*

On March 7 along with Companies A and C, the men of Company B marched five miles to Vaucouleurs where they were loaded once again into the 40 hommes, 8 chevaux railcars for the long trip to Le Mans and eventually home. The uneventful trip was made more tolerable by the "rescue" of many bottles of champagne from a damaged boxcar nearby.

The 103rd Engineers were in the Le Mans forwarding camp for more than a month. All their equipment had been turned in and although they built an auditorium for the YMCA and worked on several other buildings, they still had plenty of time on their hands. There was, as always, drilling, marching and inspections, but they were now essentially tourists in a country they had helped to save. Ed had plenty of time to draw portraits of local people, foreign fighters and wounded soldiers; he even had to buy additional sketchbooks in Le Mans.

Café du Pilier Rouge
Le Mans

House of the Court Executioner about A.D. 1430

No 25

French Hospital Train Attendant.

← **142** *Café du Pilier Rouge*
↑ **143** *Hospital Train Attendant*

Side Show, Le Mans

144 *Side Show*

A Nun

+ No 20

145 *Nun*

Wounded Yanks taking in the sights.

+ No 22

146 *Wounded Yanks*

147 *Senegalese Trooper*

148 *Croix de Guerre*

149 *Woman, Le Mans*

Comin' Home.

On April 20 most of the 103rd Engineers boarded the *SS Finland* in the port of St. Nazaire for the trip home. The voyage was quiet and uneventful. There was little to do and the sense of excitement of going to war that had pervaded their last ocean voyage was missing. The great adventure, that had so energized them a year ago, was now over. A sense of let-down mingled with feelings of anticipation.

They arrived at Pier No. 3 in Hoboken, New Jersey on the morning of May 1, 1919. There was a large, enthusiastic crowd there to greet them with cake, candy and ice cream. The soldiers – soon to be civilians – were transferred to Fort Dix, New Jersey, where they lived for the next two weeks while they were processed.

← **150** *Comin' Home*

On May 15 two million people lined the streets of Philadelphia to welcome home the Iron Division. The reviewing stand at Independence Hall was decorated with bunting and surmounted by the Mayor and Governor in top hats. Eighteen thousand soldiers marched down Broad Street; rifles, with bayonets fixed, on their shoulders, past banners with names such as Château Thierry and Argonne hanging from balconies. They marched with an ease and confidence of those who had done the job asked of them, and had done it well. Lining the streets they saw adoring throngs, many younger than themselves and were reminded of the fresh youthfulness they had possessed, when going to war was just a dream. Now they were men and now they were ready to get on with the rest of their lives. They were discharged from the army on Friday, May 16, 1919 and went home.

← 151 *Soldiers in the Mud*

AFTERWORD

After the war Ed returned to his family home on N. 56th St. but soon he moved out and had an apartment of his own. He enrolled in the Pennsylvania Academy of Fine Arts and resumed his training. He studied illustration in the Brandywine tradition; his instructors were students of its founder, Howard Pyle. Pyle was a romantic and Ed found himself once again drawing knights in armor, dragons and pirates.

As a consequence of the Great War, empires were dismantled, countries abolished and new ones formed. The world of the last hundred years had disappeared and a new one had taken its place. By 1920 people were eager to put the past behind them and get on with the future. There was little interest in what happened in the war. Soldiers' stories went untold, not because they were reluctant to tell them but because no one wanted to hear them.

Ed's sketchbooks were put away. In later years he wrote stories that included his wartime experiences, but they were never illustrated with drawings done while he was overseas. His sketchbooks remained unseen for over ninety years.

His work at the Academy was exceptional and he won the Lee Prize for his figure drawing and two Cresson Scholarships for study in Europe. In 1922 he again boarded a ship headed east, this time as an artist rather than a soldier.

When Ed returned from Europe in 1924, he went to work as a book editor, putting his drawing talents on the back burner. When he was Editor-in-Chief of *The Western* he had done everything necessary to get it out to his audience. He wrote articles, edited columns, illustrated, laid out and published the magazine. Now he was doing the same at Penn Publishing Company, but this time for whole books. During this period he wrote his first novel, *The Gray Beginning,* which got noticed and established him as a writer, before he was recognized as an artist.

At the age of 31, he moved from Penn Publishing to Macrae-Smith and within two years, was their vice president. Here he wrote his second novel, *The Lean Twilight* but this time he sold it to Charles Scribner's Sons, a major New York publisher.

He had been writing short stories for the *Scribner's Magazine* for the previous three years. In 1929 in addition to his job at Macrae-Smith, he also joined Scribner's as an illustrator and in 1930 succeeded Rockwell Kent as the house artist, a position he held for the next ten years. While at Scribner's, Ed did illustrations and covers for several of their books, among them Fitzgerald's *Tender is the Night*, Hemingway's *Green Hills of Africa* and Marjorie Kinnan Rawlings' *The Yearling*.

One of the stories Ed wrote for Scribner's in 1926, *All the Boats to Build,* deals with a veteran who is apparently suffering from what we now call Post Traumatic Stress Disorder. He nearly shoots his girlfriend and her lover but eventually finds solace in boat building. *Plenty of Seconds* is about a chef who joins the army as a cook; *The Infantry Wanted a Bridge* about his time in Fismes and *Call it a Day,* the story of a corporal and his infantry squad in battle. It is probably based on the exploits of the 110th and 111th Infantry from the Marne to the Ourcq. Ed illustrated this story with new drawings, none of them derived from the sketches he did during the war. In 1935 Ed wrote *When Spring Brings Back*, a short story in which a veteran revisits the scene of one of his battles with his wife and friends and remembers the horrors; they are callous, uninterested and don't understand, but he bonds with a French cabbie who is a veteran. The story won the O'Henry Prize in 1935, along with Thomas Wolfe and William Saroyan.

Scribner's Magazine ceased publication in 1939, but Ed continued to do illustation work for them and for numerous other book publishers on a freelance basis. Just before the start of the Second World War he returned to the Philadelphia Academy of Fine Arts as a teacher.

Ever since the Wright Brothers took to the air Ed had been fascinated with aviation. In 1911 he did a booklet similar to his auto racing ones about a daring pilot in a very early aircraft. His passion continued and he did several airplane books for Macrae-Smith and, at the outbreak of World War II, wrote and illustrated several more. *The New Alphabet of Aviation, On Winds of Freedom* and *The Alphabet of the Army* were all published during the war.

Ed continued to receive assignments well into the 1960's and these, along with his stories, poetry and teaching filled his time. Except for his two visits to France, Ed stayed near Philadelphia for most of his life. At the age of 78, Ed and his wife, Barbara, moved to Boothbay Harbor, Maine, near their only child, Ned. Ed and Barbara died within two weeks of each other in 1977.

Ned inherited the cardboard boxes containing his father's papers and carried them with him as he moved, occasionally examining their contents, until 2009.

In his career, Edward Shenton wrote twelve books of his own, and illustrated at least 135 written by others. He had nearly one hundred stories and many poems published in such magazines as *The Saturday Evening Post* and *The New Yorker*. He even wrote the lyrics for a cantata performed by the Philadelphia Symphony.

He was a commercial illustrator rather than a fine artist and the vast majority of his work was done for hire, except for the sketches and drawings he did while in the army from 1917 to 1919.

Edward Shenton fought for his country when it called and acquitted himself well. In a very real way he fulfilled his childhood dream of a great knightly errand accomplished with his closest friends.

Edward Shenton (1895-1977)

LIST OF DRAWINGS
The Early Years

001 *Battling Ships and Drowning Sailors*
6 ¾" x 4 ½" 172 mm x 114 mm
This and the drawing below are contained in a neat black notebook, about 5" x 7"; inscribed inside the front cover in neat block letters is "This book drawn about nine years ago. Oct. 1914."

002 *Teddy Roosevelt*
4" x 4 ½" 102 mm x 114 mm
The captions on these sketches read, "Roosevelt Colnl of Rough Riders" and "Teddy leading the charge on San Juan Hill."

003 *Sir Nigel Loring*
4 ¼" x 2 ¾" 108 mm x 70 mm
In an article entitled "The Book Illustration of Edward Shenton", Henry Pitz, a friend and contemporary, wrote that Shenton drew hundreds of scenes of "medieval carnage," but few have survived.

004 *Graham of Claverhouse*
5 ½" x 4 ½" 140 mm x 114 mm
Ed probably read Ian Maclaren's book, *Graham of Claverhouse*, which was published in 1907.

005 *Around the Repair Camps*
10" x 4" 254 mm x 102 mm
Ed drew at least nine booklets. They explore all aspects of motor racing in the early teens, including the starting lineup for the first Indianapolis 500 race in 1911.

006 **Simplex Cars on Road and Track,** *April 1911 Cover*
10" x 4" 254 mm x 102 mm

Many of the drawings in this issue were given the photo credit of A. B. Allen, but all were obviously drawn by Ed. On the cover is the number 22, Simplex "Red Devil" piloted by the Shenton brothers.

007 Motor Car Record, *Vol. II*
5" x 4" 127 mm x 102 mm
This booklet consists of portraits of six famous auto racers of the time including Ray Harroun, winner of the first Indianapolis 500, and Louis Chevrolet.

008 Les Magasin des Follies
4.5" x 8" 114 mm x 203 mm

009 *The Queen's Revenge*
4.5" x 8" 114 mm x 203 mm

010 *A Four-Day Beard and a Boil*
4" x 6 ¾" 102 mm x 171 mm
In June, school was out and Ed and Don were sailing on the "Yacht" Mable with a high school friend named Robert Whetstone. It looks like they were letting go of the stress of the school year.

011 *Yacht Mable*
6 ¾" x 4" 171 mm x 102 mm
Ed and Don and "Captain" Whetstone sailed in Barnegat Bay from Toms River to Barnegat City.

012 The Western, *December 1914 Cover*
6 ¾" x 10" 171 mm x 254 mm
In the four years Ed was at West Philadelphia High School he drew at least nine covers for *The Western*, two of which were in color.

013 The Western, *April 1914 Cover*
6 ¾" x 10" 171 mm x 254 mm

014 The Western, *October 1914 Frontispiece*
6 ¾" x 8 ¾" 171 mm x 222 mm
This is one of my favorite drawings.

015 *Rogues Gallery*
6" x 4 ½" 152 mm x 114 mm
Most of the portraits in the "Rogues Gallery" are of women. Each is accompanied with a short poem indicating that he knew his models.

016 *Edith Ogden*
6" x 4 ½" 152 mm x 114 mm

017 *Don Shenton*
6" x 4 ¾" 152 mm x 121 mm
This portrait of Don was done in the summer of 1915 just before he went away to Penn State. He would have graduated from college in the spring of 1919 had not the war intervened.

018 *Famous Simplex Pilot Retires*
10" x 4" 254 mm x 102 mm

Enlistment

019 *The Skull*
4 ¾" x 5 ½" 121 mm x 140 mm
This drawing is the last one in the sketchbook done
at The Museum School in the winter of 1916-17. It was drawn
at a time when Ed was struggling with his own melancholy
and his decision whether or not to join the upcoming fight.

020 *Mug-Wamp*
3" x 5 ¼" 76 mm x 133 mm

021 *Mug-Wamp Goes to War*
2 ½" x 2 ½" 64 mm x 64 mm
After a winter of vacillation, "all incompleteness had been
resolved."

022 *Meade Sketchbook Cover*
8" x 5 ¼" 203 mm x 133 mm
Ed purchased various sizes of sketchbooks at Wanamaker's,
ranging in size from 4" x 7" to 9 ¼" x 11." Each sketchbook
had 24 pages of high-quality paper suitable for pencil,
ink or watercolor.

023 *Rupert Brooke*
5" x 7 ½" 127 mm x 190 mm
This book was given to Ed with the following inscription
"To Ed Shenton from Ida La P. Flint, Christmas 1917 – Over
the top with a bit of luck and give them what they deserve!
Merry Christmas!"

Learning to Be a Soldier
Camp Meade

024 *July 4th Pup Tent*
7 ¾" x 4 ¼" 197 mm x 108 mm
This sketch was done the same day they arrived at Odenton,
Maryland and may be the first drawing done at what is today
Fort Meade, home of the National Security Agency.

025 *Repairing Ventilators*
5 ¼" x 8" 133 mm x 203 mm
Each tent had a conical Sibley stove for heat, which was placed
on the ground and vented to the outside via a metal stovepipe.

026 *Johnny Armstrong with newspaper*
7 ¼" x 5" 184 mm x 127 mm

027 *Well No. 2*
7 ¾" x 5" 197 mm x 127 mm

028 *The Road Builders*

7 ¾" x 5" 197 mm x 127 mm

029 *An Engineer's Daily Drill*

3 ½" x 6" 89 mm x 152 mm

This sketchbook is entitled "Some Survey Sketches and Hiking Notes and Trench Tracings Camp Hancock Augusta Georgia."

030 *The Pick and Shovel Gang*

10" x 8 ½" 254 mm x 216 mm

This Camp Hancock drawing is in one of the three largest sketchbooks (9" x 10 ¾").

031 *The Gamblers*

7" x 5" 178 mm x 127 mm

This drawing is graphite with a watercolor wash laid over.

032 *The Kingdom of the Cook*

8 ¾" x 8 ½" 222 mm x 216 mm

A total of nineteen cooks served with Company B from the beginning of training until the end of the war. One was killed, two wounded and one gassed.

033 *Cook Tent*

7 ½" x 5" 191 mm x 127 mm

034 *The Baggage Pile*

7 ¾" x 4 ¾" 197 mm x 121 mm

This drawing was done on the engineers' last day at Camp Meade. They had spent three days packing and left for Camp Hancock in the evening. This is the last drawing in the Camp Meade sketchbook labeled "III."

Camp Hancock

035 *Company Street*

5" x 7 ¼" 127 mm x 184 mm

There are two sketchbooks with overlapping dates from Ed's first days at Camp Hancock. One, a smaller book numbered "IV", was started at Hancock (the earliest date is 9/9/17), while the other, one of the largest ones spans both Meade and Hancock. This sketch is from the larger book.

036 *Field Bakery*

7 ¾" x 5" 197 mm x 127 mm

When the division moved overseas, the portable bakery went along. The soldiers behind the lines got fresh bread on a regular basis while for the front line combat troops it was a rare luxury.

037 *Survey Party*

3 ¾" x 6 ¼" 95 mm x 159 mm

038 *Bomb Proof Trench Work*

7 ½" x 5" 191 mm x 127 mm

This drawing was done at Camp Meade on August 1, 1917, when the men had been in training less than one month.

039 *Napping in the Trenches*
7 ¼" x 5 ½" 184 mm x 140 mm
This sketch was done in April, 1918.

040 *Shooting Silhouettes*
7 ½" x 5 ¼" 190 mm x 133 mm
This drawing is from a sketchbook dated April, 1918.
Many of the sketches in this book show soldiers practicing
with their rifles.

041 *Two riflemen*
8" x 5 ½" 203 mm x 140 mm
This was the last drawing done before they left for overseas.

042 *Thirty Second Sketch*
7 ½" x 4 ¾" 190 mm x 121 mm
In many sketches Ed did a very quick line drawing laying out
the composition and then filled in the details and shading
later. He used this technique throughout his time in the army.
Some sketches show up multiple times, in sketchbooks,
as loose pages, and eventually some were published in
The Philadelphia Record.

043 *Artillery Range Hike*
8" x 5 ½" 203 mm x 140 mm
The company spent from April 15 to 17, 1918 on the artillery
range at Spirit Creek, Georgia.

044 *Our Tent*
8" x 5 ¼" 203 mm x 133 mm
This and several adjacent drawings were most likely done
at Spirit Creek.

045 *The Signaler*
7 ¼" x 4 ½" 184 mm x 114 mm
This watercolor was done at Camp Meade on August 16,
1917.

046 *The Gun Control*
9 ½" x 8" 241 mm x 203 mm
This watercolor shows an officer relaying orders to a ghostly
gun crew (outlined in pencil) from someone in a bunker
wearing a headset. It was done at Camp Hancock in
September of 1917.

047 *The View from My Cot by Day*
6 ¾" x 4 ¾" 171 mm x 121 mm
This Camp Hancock drawing is in one of the three largest
sketchbooks (9" x 10 ¾").

048 *Things Are on the Mend!*
10 ½" x 8 ½" 267 mm x 216 mm

049 *Buy a Bond*
7 ½" x 5 ½" 190 mm x 140 mm
In the last sketchbook he used before they went overseas, Ed
did at least four dramatic sketches for bond drives.

050 *The Sunny South*

2" x 4 ¼" 51 mm x 108 mm

This cartoon, along with # 51, 52 and 53 were published in Volume 6, number 9 of *The Western* in May of 1918. Called the Service Number, Ed also draw its rather dramatic cover. The issue contains a list of over 250 boys from West Philly High who served in the War.

051 *Charlie Ruff*

2 ½" x 3 ¾" 64 mm x 95 mm

Charlie Ruff was one of the original sixteen who joined with Ed. He is shown here with a portable plane table for surveying.

052 *Zirkman and Lauber*

3" x 3 ¾" 76 mm x 95 mm

Both Arthur Zirkman and Graham Lauber joined the army with Ed. This incident refers to the time when they were at the artillery range and food was rationed.

053 *Harold Menaugh and Doc Thompson*

3 ½" x 3" 89 mm x 76 mm

Harold Menaugh was one of Ed's oldest friends. He was one of the fantasy drivers in the *Simplex Cars on Road and Track* booklets and worked with him on *The Western*.
Doc Thompson joined with Ed in April, 1917.

054 *Xmas Dinner in the Army*

1 ¼" x 8" 260 mm x 203 mm

Corporal Pat Metelski, one of *The Western* correspondents, said that their "Xmas dinner would make Solomon's Feast look like a free lunch counter."

055 *Winter is Here*

10 ¼" x 7 ½" 260 mm x 190 mm

This winter sketchbook also incudes drawings of tents in the snow, gloved sentries and soldiers in trench coats standing in the rain.

056 *Captain Ryan*

3 ½" x 6 ¼" 89 mm x 159 mm

Captain Ryan is mentioned by name in at least one other book about the AEF.

057 *Six Inches of Steel for a Hun*

6 ½" x 4" 165 mm x 102 mm

058 *Hand Grenade Throwing*

9 ½" x 7" 241 mm x 178 mm

059 *Firing a Stokes Trench Mortar*

8" x 5" 203 mm x 127 mm

This image is from one of the larger sketchbooks.

060 *Boxing in the Grove*
6 ¾" x 4 ¾" 171 mm x 121 mm

061 *Lettering the Combat Wagon*
7 ¼" x 5" 184 mm x 127 mm

Going to War
Journey to France

062 *Battleship*
4 ½" x 2 ¼" 114 mm x 57 mm

063 *On the Rail*
3 ½" x 4 ½" 89 mm x 114 mm

This small drawing, is from a sketchbook that Ed used on the trip back to the U. S. in 1919. We have not found one for his trip to France in 1918 and it would be surprising if he did no drawings on this voyage. Perhaps there is still a lost sketchbook.

064 *Something Spotted*
4" x 4 ¾" 102 mm x 121 mm

065 *What is it?*
4" x 5" 102 mm x 127 mm

066 *Calais Rest Camp*
11" x 5 ¼" 279 mm x 133 mm

This drawing is one of many loose sheets that were found among Ed`s papers. It was done in pencil with the text copied over in ink. There are many drawings of this style, several of which were first drawn in a sketchbook and re-drawn at a later time. Could the original of this drawing be in a sketchbook that also contains images from the voyage over?

067 *Mostly Billets Sketchbook*
4 ½" x 6 ¼" 114 mm x 159 mm

This is the first sketchbook Ed used in France. The first two pencil sketches in this book are truncated on the outer edge, while the rest comfortably fit the page. It was obviously a 6" x 9" sketchbook cut in half to be more easily carried. Artists did the same during the Second World War.

068 *A Farm in Crémarest*
5 ¾" x 4 ¼" 146 mm x 108 mm

The name of this farm has been obscured by the sensor, but is still readable. Several drawings done at this time have the names of locations crossed out.

069 *Our First Billet in France*
6" x 3 ½" 152 mm x 89 mm

This is most likely Crémarest. By this time Ed had learned not to use town names on his drawings.

070 *Cootie Shed*
4 ½" x 3 ¼" 114 mm x 83 mm
This drawing was done in early June, 1918.

071 *Gas Mask*
5" x 9" 127 mm x 229 mm
This sketch was done at Camp Hancock, probably in the spring of 1918 in a large (9" x 11") sketchbook cut in half.

072 *Cathedral at Crémarest*
4 ½" x 6" 114 mm x 152 mm
The Church of Our Lady of Grace in Crémarest was built in the fourteenth century and the tower was added in the sixteenth to shelter the citizens from the marauding English. Ed drew this sketch in the twentieth and the church looks exactly the same in a photo taken in the twenty first.

Charly-sur-Marne

073 *Resting after our Train Ride Through France*
4 ½" X 5 ¼" 114 mm x 133 mm
This sketch was done at the train station at La Ferté -Gaucher after their trip from Crémarest.

074 *Our Second Billet*
6" x 3 ¾" 152 mm x 95 mm
La Courterie

075 *Our Third Billet, an Old Château*
5 ¾" x 4 ¼" 146 mm x 108 mm
Charly-sur-Marne

076 *Front Line Trenches*
6 ¼" x 3 ¾" 159 mm x 95 mm
This sketch was done at Camp Hancock. Drawing sketches of the trenches they built in France could have gotten him in real trouble.

Saint-Agnan

077 *On the Line!*
4 ½" x 5 ½" 114 mm x 140 mm
This page was loose among Ed's papers. It is the same size as the half-sketchbook with images of the battles at Saint-Agnan and Fismes and may have been the title page of this book, which has only sixteen of the usual twenty-four pages.

078 *Camion*
7 ¾" x 4 ¼" 184 mm x 108 mm
The sketch of this Standard B "Liberty" truck was done at Camp Meade; many were shipped to France. Sixteen men sat in the back; the ride was rough and sleep difficult.

079 *Possibly Montigny-lès-Condé*
5 ½" x 4 ½" 140 mm x 114 mm
This typical French village may be Montigny-lès-Condé.

The page appears to have been torn from the "On the Line!" sketchbook and the buildings closely resemble those I saw in the village using Google Maps.

080 *Front Line Trench, Morning*
5 ½" x 4 ½" 140 mm x 114 mm
"Someone had hurriedly dug a drainage ditch on the side of a hill further up the line. The general called it a trench and put us into it. He said, 'When Fritz comes along, tell him to wait. Paris is crowded now." This quote is from a letter Ed wrote to *The Western* after the battle.

081 *Where'd That Un Go?*
4 ½" x 5 ¼" 114 mm x 133 mm
This drawing shows a scared young man who has left his rifle on the bank outside his shallow trench. This drawing catches the moment when for Ed, the war became more than an adventure.

082 *Front Line Trench, Evening*
5 ½" x 4 ½" 140 mm x 114 mm
"Jerry didn't come himself; that is – all the way! He stopped on the hill opposite and in some towns below us and sent up his cards. I remember the first shell that exploded in the barbed wire. We thought it was a good joke. I got out my watch. We wanted to see what time the first one arrived. No one remembers when the second one came. I never found my watch. I thought I put it in my pocket, but I guess I threw it at the shell. From then on no one stopped to count." From Ed's *Western* letter.

083 *This is Home*
4 ½" x 5 ¾" 114 mm x 146 mm
Ed's "home" in the Bois de Rougis from July 16 to 18 was in a hole next to a tree.

084 *Doc Thompson*
4" x 4 ¼" 102 mm x 108 mm
Doc Thompson "received a section of pig-iron in a very tender portion of his anatomy, and Freddie Street collected a little in his ankle."

085 *Freddie Street*
4 ¼" x 3 ¾" 108 mm x 95 mm

Fismes

086 *Street in a Ruined Town*
6" x 5 ¼" 152 mm x 133 mm
This sketch is in the "On the Line!" sketchbook, which contains images of the battles of St. Agnan and Fismes. It may be of one of the towns between Montigny and Moulins, perhaps Monthurel or Connigis. The name has been erased by a censor and written over.

087 *Fourth Billet*
4 ½" x 5 ½" 140 mm x 114 mm

088 *Burying Detail*
5 ½" x 5" 140 mm x 127 mm
This graphite sketch was one of three on a larger sheet entitled "Moulins" in ink lettering.

089 *"B" Company Kitchen*
4 ½" x 6" 114 mm x 152 mm
This sketch was most likely done at Crémarest where the engineers were provided with a British kitchen wagon.

090 *Dead Germans in a Wheat Field*
5 ¾" x 3 ¾" 146 mm x 95 mm
This sketch from the "On the Line!" book was later completely re-done for the "Moulins" sheet.

091 *Along the Vesle*
7 ¼" x 5 ¼" 184 mm x 133 mm
This drawing is one of two on a larger sheet lettered in ink. The other drawing is a French soldier with a machine gun on his shoulder. The entire sheet is 13 1/2" x 9 1/4," 343 mm x 235 mm.

092 *German Shells Bursting in a Town*
5 ¾" x 4 ¼" 146 mm x 108 mm
This sketch of Fismes was most likely done from Mont-Saint-Martin early on the morning of August 6, before they moved off to Resson Farm and dug in. The untouched town hall is visible in the center.

093 *The Hun Shelling an American Battery of 75's*
5 ½" x 4 ½" 140 mm x 114 mm
This loose sketch is likely one of the pages missing from the "On the Line!" sketchbook. It may have been done at Resson Farm.

094 *Homes No. 10 and 11 at Resson Farm and Les Petites Chezelles Farm*
4 ½" x 6" 114 mm x 152 mm
These drawings appeared in *The Philadelphia Record* on November 10, 1918 along with a caption indicating that Home No 10 was a shell hole and No 11 the end of a trench. The upper drawing is from Resson Farm and shows Ed's home after two days of improvements. The lower is of their hastily constructed dugout at Les Petites Chezelles Farm the next day.

095 *Hasty Footbridge*
7 ¼" x 3 ¾" 184 mm x 95 mm
Part of a larger sheet with three drawings.

096 *Engineer Dugout*
5 ¾" x 6 ¼" 146 mm x 159 mm
This and # 97 are the same subject done at different times. # 96 was probably done in Fismes, during the battle. It takes up two pages in the "On the Line!" sketchbook; # 97 was a new composition on loose sheet with ink lettering.

097 *Engineer's P. C. in Fismes*
9 ¼" x 12 ¾" 235 mm x 324 mm
In many cases Ed redrew a sketch he had done in one of his sketchbooks in a larger format with carefully done lettering in ink.

098 *The City Hall after Jerry Finished the Prelude*
4" x 6" 102 mm x 152 mm
This drawing and # 98 were both bound in the "On the Line!" sketchbook, with two pages between.

099 *The Town Hall a Week Later*
4 ½" x 5 ¾" 114 mm x 146 mm
This drawing and # 97 were both done after August 15.

100 *Runners in Fismes*
12 ½" x 8 ½" 318 mm x 216 mm
One of the larger loose sheets with ink lettering.

101 *Gas*
5" x 5 ½" 127 mm x 140 mm
This sketch was done on a sheet of paper never bound into a sketchbook.

102 *Camouflage on a Road*
5 ½" x 4 ½" 140 mm x 114 mm
This drawing is probably from the "On the Line!" sketchbook.

103 *The Reading Room*
6" x 4 ½" 152 mm x 114 mm

104 *Mendy Finds a Magazine*
4 ½" x 5 ½" 114 mm x 140 mm

105 *Bridge Across the Vesle Below Magneaux*
13 ½" x 6 ¾" 343 mm x 171 mm
On a separate sheet, carefully lettered in ink

106 *In the Cave at Villette*
6 ¾" x 5" 171 mm x 127 mm
On a separate sheet, carefully lettered in ink

107 *Going Out of the Marne Sector*
12 ¼" x 9 ¼" 311 mm x 235 mm
On a separate sheet, carefully lettered in ink

Argonne

108 *Doughboy*
5 ¼" x 5 ¼" 133 mm x 133 mm
From the "On the Line" sketchbook.

109 *Rabbits and Offs*
9" x 8" 229 mm x 203 mm
Done at Bettancourt between September 12 and 15.

110 *First Sunday Behind the Lines*
5 ½" x 4 ½" 140 mm x 114 mm
This loose sketch appears to have been torn from a half-sketchbook. There are only two sketchbooks, both cut in half, that date from France before the Armistice but many loose sketches.

111 *Gas and Wire*
5" x 5 ¾" 127 mm x 146 mm
The red pencil work on this loose drawing could have possibly been done after the original drawing.

112 *American Ambulance*
7 ½" x 5 ½" 190 mm x 140 mm
This drawing was done at Camp Hancock.

113 *Ration Wagon*
5" x 3 ¾" 127 mm x 95 mm
This loose sketch was probably once in a sketchbook.

114 *French Howitzer*
5" x 3 ½" 127 mm x 89 mm
This model 1918 Schneider 155 millimeter howitzer would have been the artillery that traveled on the newly repaired road in the Argonne. It is from a group of loose sheets, all of them with three punched holes. Although the images are from distant dates (one from Crémarest and one from Bettancourt-la-Longue) the location of the holes on the sheets correspond.

115 *Prisoner of War*
3 ½" x 5" 89 mm x 127 mm
This is one of thirty loose sketches with the same proportion. Most appear to have been drawn after the Armistice as they are of civilians, prisoners or wounded servicemen. They all have one cut edge, several with the exactly same profile. Most of them are numbered.

116 *Doughboys Bringing Back Wounded*
12" x 8" 205 mm x 203 mm
From a large, loose sheet with ink lettering.

117 *Baby Tanks at Varennes*
6 ½" x 3 ½" 159 mm x 89 mm
Ed refers to these Renault FT-17 as "baby tanks" as they were much smaller than the British Mark Vs. He saw them at Varennes after they were repaired.

118 *Feldbahnhof*

6 ¾" x 4 ¾" 171 mm x 121 mm

Feldbahnhof translates as field train station.

Metz

119 *Vigneulles*

7 ¼" x 4 ¾" 185 mm x 121 mm

These two views of Vigneulles were found loose in a box among Ed's papers. They were probably from the same sketchbook, possibly the one entitled "Fini la Guerre."

120 *Vigneulles Ruins*

7 ¼" x 4 ¾" 185 mm x 121 mm

The town, which had been in German hands for most of the war, was bombarded and captured by Americal Troops shortly before Company B moved there on October 28.

121 *Armistice at Commercy*

4 ½" x 5 ½" 114 mm x 140 mm

The caption of this sketch indicates that Ed was in Commercy on November 11 while Company B was billeted in Vigneulles. Another drawing is dated November 12 is from Haumont, nearly 40 miles away. It seems that Ed was on the move when the war ended.

122 *Germans at Haumont*

not available

Haumont was destroyed in the battle of Verdun in 1916 and was never rebuilt. It is deemed a "village that died for France." It is still administered by a council in a neighboring town.
I copied this image from a 1919 newspaper, but did not see the original.

FINI LA GUERRE!

123 *Fini la Guerre!*

7 ¼" x 4 ¾" 185 mm x 121 mm

This title page was signed by 1st lieutenant G. D. Dixon Jr. with his "OK" indicating that it has passed his test as censor.

124 *Hattonchâtel Church*

4 ¾" x 6 ½" 120 mm x 165 mm

The church at Hattonchâtel had been damaged during the bombardment of 1914 when the Germans first occupied the town and maybe also when it was liberated in September of 1918.

125 *The Rat Hunter*

4 ½" x 6 ½" 114 mm x 165 mm

After the Armistice, Ed became more prolific with his drawings as he had much more time on his hands.

126 *Keystones*
3 ½" x 6 ¼" 89 mm x 159 mm

127 *Chevrons*
3 ½" x 6" 89 mm x 152 mm

128 *Old Joe*
2 ¼" x 4 ½" 57 mm x 114 mm

129 *Uruffe Washerwoman*
4" x 4 ½" 102 mm x 114 mm

130 *Rail Yards at Commercy*
7 ¼" x 4 ¾" 185 mm x 121 mm

131 *Mongolian at Neufchâteau*
5" x 7 ½" 127 mm x 190 mm
Twelve miles south is the market town of Neufchâteau, but unlike Uruffe it had a café and some nightlife which attracted the bored soldiers. Throughout the war there was a shortage of truck drivers and often Vietnamese or Mongolians filled this role.

132 *Liberty Plane*
7 ¼" x 4 ¼" 185 mm x 108 mm
This Airco DH 4 was a daytime bomber flown by both American and British pilots. "Liberty" may refer to its 400 horsepower Liberty engine. The U. S. 96th Aero Squadron was equipped with DH 4's at Colombey-les-Belles in 1918.

133 *Night Bomber*
7 ½" x 5 1/8" 190 mm x 130 mm
The plane Ed drew is not, as the caption says, a French bomber, but rather a Royal Aircraft Factory F.E. 2b night bomber, which were only flown by British pilots. Colombey-les-Belles Airdrome was a large AEF depot where squadrons of pilots received their equipment before being deployed to forward units.

134 *Railway Gun*
5 1/8" x 2 5/8" 130 mm x 67 mm
This 320 mm (12") French railroad gun was one of the largest caliber cannons used in the war. These battleship guns were mounted on heavy railroad cars; they threw a high explosive shell weighing 850 pounds over twenty miles.

135 *Infantry*
3 ¾" x 6 ¼" 95 mm x 159 mm
There are a total of ten drawings in this "who won the war" series. In addition to those below there are: MP, aviator, first aid man and truck driver. They were all done after Ed arrived in Le Mans.

136 *Artillery*
3 ¾" x 6 ¼" 95 mm x 159 mm

137 *Engineer*
3 ¾" x 6 ¼" 95 mm x 159 mm

138 *Stevedore*
3 ¾" x 6 ¼" 95 mm x 159 mm

139 *Cook*
3 ¾" x 6 ¼" 95 mm x 159 mm

140 *Stable Rat*
3 ¾" x 6 ¼" 95 mm x 159 mm

141 *40 Hommes et 8 Chevaux*
7 ¼" x 5" 185 mm x 127 mm
This could have been sketched from inside a boxcar.

142 *Café du Pilier Rouge*
3 ¾" x 6 3/8" 95 mm x 162 mm
All eight of the following drawings were done by Ed when
he was in Le Mans. One can still eat at the Café du Pilier
Rouge today.

143 *Hospital Train Attendant*
3 ½" x 5" 89 mm x 127 mm

144 *Side Show*
3 ½" x 5 ½" 89 mm x 140 mm

145 *Nun*
3 ½" x 5" 89 mm x 127 mm

146 *Wounded Yanks*
3 ½" x 5" 89 mm x 127 mm

147 *Senegalese Trooper*
4" x 5 ¼" 102 mm x 133 mm

148 *Croix de Guerre*
3 ¾" x 4" 95 mm x 102 mm

149 *Woman, Le Mans*
3 ¾" x 3 ¾" 95 mm x 95 mm

150 *Comin' Home*
4" x 5 1/8" 102 mm x 130 mm

151 *Soldiers in the Mud*
6" x 7 ¾" 152 mm x 197 mm
It is not clear where or when this drawing was done,
but it captures what a soldiers' life was like.

Corp E. Shenton
Co B 103rd Engrs
28th Div A.E.F.
France